TRANSFORMATION FROM WITHIN

A journey of hope and resilience

SUBHANA HYE

Acknowledgements

I thank Allah (swt) my Almighty God
for making my dream come true.

This book is dedicated to my mother and my late father, without you this wouldn't have been possible. Thank you for giving me the basic life lessons on hope and resilience. I live by your example, and I cherish every moment that I have and had with you.

I have many wonderful people that I am grateful to, below are a few.

I would like to thank my friends and family.
Special thanks to my husband, Adem Ibrahim for
being kind and supportive throughout this journey.

Special thanks to Beth Sear also known as my
'brain twin' for encouraging me to start writing,
for always being my number one supporter.

Thanks to my HEE Book club – Christine Strickett, Louise Brooker and special thanks to Shreya Chandarana and Natalie Moyanah for reading my first edits and putting up with me and sticking by me for the days where I just didn't think I could carry on. Not only are you all great sports to be around, but you also showed me how to prosper intellectually and have a different perspective.

Thanks to Annie Mirza, for introducing
me to the world of book writing.

Thanks to Nadia Alam, my life coach, you have been
my light in days where it didn't seem possible. I thank
you for every piece of wisdom you have taught me.

Finally, I thank Aji R. Michael for making this all
possible - from having a virtual call that was the beginning
of an idea; you made the dream come alive, you are an
inspiration not only to me but to everyone around you.

I would also like to give special thanks to my editor, Kemi Oyesola
for being so wonderful, for pushing me to my limit. There were
days where your feedback was hard to digest, but I respect your
approach, and your ethos on creating EXCELLENCE!
Thank you for being the amazing human being you are.

Transformation From Within

A journey of hope and resilience

Contents Page:

INTRODUCTION

Not everyone can tell their story. Not everyone wants to tell their story. Not everyone who tells their story can tell it in full. For some, they are still hurting and are not yet healed. For others, they have tucked the pain away never to visit it again as a way of coping and moving on. They cannot move on even if they think they have.

I fall in the category of those who can tell their story but not in full. However, one thing I promise you will find in my book, *'Transformation from Within: a journey of hope and resilience'* is reality. I want you to be moved to becoming a stronger person again, I want you to find hope, to commit to finding hope again.

I set out to write a book for my South East Asian community because it helps greatly when you know someone else knows what you are going through, have been through and how to help you on the journey to transformation – I hope this will be your goal even if it is not - right now.

So, look out for bits and pieces of my story interspersed throughout the chapters of the book and at the end of each chapter, I will go into a bit more detail about certain aspects of my story and as well as a case study or two.

Enjoy, as I invite you into my life.

Stay strong.

Be kind to yourself.

Subhana Hye

CHAPTER ONE
LEARN TO DODGE THE BULLET

"When all your dreams and hopes are shattered, what is the best way to help yourself? The answer is 'you'; look at you and remember only you can take care of and nurture yourself."

M ost people in life go through the moment that changes everything, a moment where you 'narrowly escape' a situation – *dodge the bullet* as they say. That was me. It seems like a lifetime ago, yet the memories remain vividly clear. I have been there where I narrowly escaped and saved myself. How I fought against the odds, against all the cultural norms and values. This is my story and how I 'barely escaped' one predicament after another, which led to transforming my life in its entirety.

My interest in Personal Development started many years ago, but in 2015, after walking out of a toxic marriage, I decided to work towards my journey of personal transformation. It was like a spiritual journey. I wanted to take charge of my life especially my mental wellbeing. I was looking for answers and a way to heal so I could rebuild my life. When all your dreams and hopes are shattered, what is the best way to help yourself? The answer is 'you'; look at you and remember only you can take care of and nurture yourself. But remember that having faith will help you achieve as you take steps on the journey of healing and transformation. So, do not allow discouragement to assail your mind, hold on when the going gets tough. Hold on.

Before I dive into how you can get to a better place and be grateful, mindful and find purpose, I want to share the moments that caused me to realise the breakeven point, the moment when I realised that something needs to be done and needs to be done now! Not later but now. For me, that moment was when I first experienced a 'mental breakdown;' I was hyperventilating so much I could not remember where I was; all I remember was darkness, and I was all alone. That is when I realised that I was in turmoil, and in a toxic marriage. A relationship, which was unhealthy, unkind, and most importantly, I was in a relationship where I felt unloved.

Everyone will have their own meaning of what a 'toxic marriage' is, and it will differ from person to person, but for me, this is what a toxic marriage means:

T – stands for **Trauma**. From the beginning till the end, it was a traumatic experience, from the moment I wake up I see trauma and till the moment I go to sleep. It was such a horrible experience; I felt confined; an experience I will never wish upon anyone. It's only now that I can put a name to what I was going through. Trauma.

Trauma can be emotive, a form of emotional abuse, for example constantly being shouted and screamed at, belittled, non-stop verbal abuse; sometimes you might feel it would never end. For me, it got to a point where I became numb, I stopped feeling, I stopped hearing myself. I was living but I didn't feel anything. It all became passive, and anything I would say or do would become a trigger. Should I stay silent?

Silence was the only way my day would pass with my mind still intact somewhat. My tears stopped, the person that I was - happy, cheerful, and full of life - no longer existed. I didn't recognise the person that I was becoming, I wasn't me anymore. I had slowly been changing into someone I did not know.

O – stands for **Overwhelmed**. To put it simply, sometimes it felt like it was too much to manage. There never seemed to be an end to the arguments. It was on repeat. It felt like I was on a rollercoaster of stress, anxiety, guilt, and fear.

X – stands for **X-ed Out** physically, emotionally, and mentally. I was slowly becoming a shadow of myself. I no longer smiled neither did I take care of myself. I was busy protecting me from being abused and putting up defences against the oppressor. I watched my life change little by little - just like that, in a blink of an eye, I was out of it. I was in disbelief, yet the reality of the situation didn't sink in, because being married and living with a man for the first time in my life was all new for me. Part of me thought, this is what married life is, or was it what I was made to believe it to be?

I – stands for **Isolated**. My marriage was such a lonely place, I felt far away from my loved ones and isolated in my mind from the world.

C – stands for **Confusion**. No one gets married with the hope that their marriage would fail, no one. I was conflicted with emotion, societal pressure, the embarrassment I would suffer of a failed marriage and its offshoots. I was confused about what my life's vision was in relation to my reality. They were not the same in any way.

I am finally ready to share my journey and life experiences. How I dodged the bullet by walking out of this toxic marriage and saved myself from heartache. I have been putting this on hold for a while, but now, I want to share with you my journey of hope and resilience.

My life has not been a comfortable ride, but it has been an exciting one, to say the least. Throughout the difficult times, I didn't realise it was important to find myself and my purpose. I hope this book will give you the help and vision that you need. I also hope it will aid those of you who are in similar situations in life and are able to resonate with me.

In this book I share where I came from and how I transformed myself after experiencing some of the most challenging times in my life. Together we can discover how to begin your 'transformation from within,' so you can live life the best way possible.

The Dream

I had a big dream like most women: get married, have kids, buy a house, and live happily ever after. I got married with high hopes, had a big dream wedding, beautiful jewellery, and the most beautifully embroidered dress with pearls, and beads. I know this sounds like a cliché, but I always wanted a 'princessy' type wedding. I remember when I first saw Kate Middleton's bouquet, perfect white bouquet with white roses and lilies, it was classy, and elegant. (I gave Kate's bouquet picture to my florist, ensuring she made the perfect Royalty bouquet for me).

In all honesty it wasn't all about the 'big wedding' it was more about the type of person that I would like to marry one day. Someone that I would call my friend, someone that I can have a laugh with, not only talk about the serious stuff. Someone who valued and respected me. It was never about how much money, or what type of job they had. I just wanted to get married so that I can start a new chapter in my life.

Bangladeshi families are huge families, and I was looking forward to that, I wanted to get married into a big family. I wanted a marriage that was a partnership, someone that I really get along with. For me 'personality' was important.

But it didn't feel that way after I got married, quite the contrary. Thinking life will work out exactly as my dream and everything fall magically into place, I focused on this being the only right path to take. I am sure you have all been there, where you feel trapped in a dead-end job or relationship; things do not seem to be working out. You may continue with life and go along with it, but eventually you realise that you're just unhappy, and you just don't know where to go or how to get your life back on track.

So, after my toxic marriage ended, I decided to travel. I got involved with various charities, spent time with friends and family, enrolled on different courses and focused on 'me.' I wanted to study, learn, and nourish my growth. I did a course on Mental Health and was fascinated with mental awareness. How does the mind work? How can you train your mind? These were all new concepts to me. I started reading books and journals. I subscribed to hundreds of YouTube channels; anything with mental health intrigued me. Not only because it was helping me figure out my own life, but it allowed me to focus on *my* interests, *my* passions. It allowed me to transform myself from a space where it was all dark, and down. Learning allowed me to live again and most importantly - I was doing this all for "me." I trained as a Neuro Linguistic Practitioner (NLP). NLP is a way of psychologically changing someone's thoughts and behaviours to help achieve the desired outcome. For me this wasn't just a new skill that I was learning, but the right step towards a life altering transformation.

It became clear to me there was a lack of representation in the personal development industry. I struggled to find a coach or therapist that looked like me and could understand what I was going through. The ones I found didn't have a clue; they did not know what an 'arranged marriage' is. Probably have read about it, but that is as far it went. That was it, that was the straw that broke the camel's back, so I made a promise to myself to help people in my community.

Touch Base

Let's start at the beginning and learn how to *dodge the bullet*. How did this all begin? How did I narrowly escape some of the darkest moments of my life?

Growing up in a Bangladeshi Muslim household, my parents brought me up in a loving environment with both Islamic and cultural values, a lot of respect, and with lots of siblings. In my family, my opinions are heard and valued. My parents gave me the best life that I could have. We travelled, visited friends and family, and enjoyed our freedom. My parents had an arranged marriage and it worked; they both understood and respected each other. Even though I was born and bred in the UK, I always knew I would have an arranged marriage; it was normal in my community, and it worked. All my sisters had arranged marriages and my cousins too. My parents were the first generation of immigrants to the UK and though they left their country behind, they did not leave their culture, family values and principles.

Let's get one thing straight too, some people assume an arranged marriage is forced but they are wrong. In fact, arranged marriages are like a 'family-and-friends-run matchmaking service.' For example, if a daughter is at an eligible age, (18 to 25 being the 'ideal' or 'prime') to get married, families and parents will start asking around the community and letting people know that their daughter is looking for a suitable husband. There is also a marriage CV or biodata, which has the bachelorette's age, name, education, occupation, both paternal and maternal grandparent's family details in Bangladesh and more. If you're wondering why there is information on the grandparents, it's to be able to trace the lineage especially because there is a caste system, for example in the Sylhet community. By sharing the name and address of the grandparents back home, people can figure out what kind of caste a bachelorette is from, and they can keep track of the family ancestry.

The 'bio-data' gets circulated and once a potential match is found, the hopeful husband and his family come to the hopeful bride's house for a meet and greet. Think of it as a big family date. The bride and groom talk in private, but some families like to have a chaperone to make sure things are kept formal and within the cultural and religious observances. The woman is not allowed to be alone with the man and it feels like the families are checking for compatibility. Not the couple. It's common for the family to look for a man with education, a good job, money, and a 'good' caste. If you are married to a man like that, you're considered one of the lucky ones. Sometimes you get to see or speak to the groom privately, other times you don't - it really depends on the family. But you *do* get pressure to make a choice which, when you're young and naïve, can be damaging. I write this now with hindsight.

I never really agreed with the interest in a man's income and caste, nor did I understand why others would think that way. Perhaps they thought that if all the necessities of life, like money and shelter are in place, then there won't be any problems. Parents assume their daughter will live comfortably, and happily with a compatible partner. Getting married is normally something that should be done with the right intentions for a happily ever after. But as I learned, sometimes, things don't always work the way you want it to, and in my case, an arranged marriage almost destroyed me. Although I was brought up with the idea of one that I will have an arranged marriage one day, I don't think I ever sat down and asked myself, 'Subhana, will you be able to go through an arranged marriage?' Could I do this? It's our culture and part of our custom and quite frankly, it had been embedded in me from a young age, however, like I said, I never gave it much thought. It was just one of those things I must do as an obedient daughter, who didn't want to upset her family. My view of marriage was to have a companion for life, someone special in your life that you can share every moment with, good and bad. Someone with whom the conversations just never stop, no matter the mood you're in, the vibe is always there. But with an arranged marriage, it's not like that, because you don't know that person at all. Yes, I did speak to him over the phone, and we exchanged messages, but we only met twice and that was while surrounded by family. So, we didn't really know each other at all, I'm sure we both probably felt the same awkward silence and shyness that comes with an arranged situation. Things shouldn't be forced, but it felt like we both were forcing each other to get to know one another.

It's always better to get to know someone before you get married, without family constantly involved. My divorce made me realise that there are a lot of things that I could have avoided to *dodge the bullet*. If I had recognised and seen the red flags perhaps, I would have acted differently in various situations. I fell into a mind trap, where I was constantly blaming myself for everything that happened to me. I felt responsible and went through a phase of self-blame, because I didn't seem to understand why I was going through all of this. *My parents' marriage had worked, why wasn't mine? What is wrong with me?*

I would ask myself these questions all the time. Sabotaging self-talk and limiting self-belief engulfed me. I thought there was something wrong with me and I was unlucky. I had friends, people around me, who would feel bad for me and say to me, "You are so unlucky, Subhana." I began to believe their narratives. Until one day, something just clicked – I had a lightbulb moment – it was when I had the panic attack, I knew then that this wasn't normal and the impact on my health was detrimental. In my heart, I knew I had had enough. At that moment in time, I knew my heart no longer wanted this marriage; I wanted a divorce.

Done!

I was done with feeling mistreated I was mentally exhausted too. I wanted my life back; I wanted *me* back. So, I focused on the person that needed to be addressed first - Me. I began a journey of understanding and how to nurture myself. It's hard not to care about what others think, especially in the Bangladeshi community which is so close knit. I knew what was coming ahead, I knew that my own community made divorced women feel ostracised. But I also knew that my life wouldn't change unless I did something. I knew there was a battle ahead. In my community, everyone knows about everyone's business. There is no safety net, and people will gossip about you before even saying hello. It can be awkward talking to your neighbours especially when they know what has happened.

I remember after my divorce I was extremely hesitant to leave my parents' house, I didn't want to see anyone from the community out of fear of what they may say. But one day, after going through everything on Netflix for three months and telling myself I needed to get my life on track, I decided to go out for a bit. My fears came true immediately.

My neighbour decided to ask me, with a smirk on her face, "Subhana, why are you staying with your Mum? Why aren't you going back to your husband?"

She feigned being in the know of the situation, but she *did* know I was hiding at my Mum's house; she knew something was wrong. I wouldn't be surprised if she had been peeking through the windows when she saw me with my car full of all I owned and my suitcases, understanding what had happened but not having the kindness or respect to ask how I am. But anyway, that is just the way it is sometimes; you can run from people, but you can't hide forever, lesson learnt.

This reminded me of the reality I already knew was ahead of me; I knew that I would have to deal with all the taboo and awkward questions, but this is the choice that I made, **'my choice'**. I was the one that had to live with a toxic person. No one else really will understand or relate no matter how much you try to explain to them.

In my community, and in fact generally, all people see is the outside. What was isolating was knowing that my community would question me and think there must be something wrong with me (after all it *is* always the woman's fault if a marriage breaks down). I convinced myself that it was true for a long time. But mentioning divorce or a difficult husband just doesn't happen in a lot of Bangladeshi Muslim communities. They think women are strong and have better coping mechanisms, which maybe we do, but to force women to cope in a toxic marriage to avoid divorce no matter what the situation or consequence, can be fatal.

Being a divorcee is *still* seen as taboo in my culture and although the rate of divorce has increased in my community; people are still old fashioned. Many still think you should do everything to sustain the marriage no matter how irrational that may be. You would hear comments like: "We've all heard of women who were murdered by their partners ... but at least they weren't divorced." That's how badly a divorce is perceived. Even though you live in a world where people are aware of what good mental health is and know the difference between a toxic and a healthy relationship, I was still bombarded with questions and felt violated. I had suffered before and was still suffering due to other people's opinions. I was the one that was unhappy in the marriage, so, what was I fighting for? Who was I doing it for? And how long can anyone survive in an empty, abusive marriage? Why did I feel the need to keep justifying and bullying myself for ending my marriage?

Finally, enough was enough. I tried to keep everyone happy by putting everyone else's needs and happiness first, by shielding my family from 'shame,' being concerned with what people will say, letting people judge whether I am a good Muslim woman or not.

It was an impossible situation and feeling like this *is* impossible to sustain; sooner or later you will crack, and that can end badly. But I was fortunate to snap out of fear before my mind was affected more severely. I knew in my heart that I could not take it anymore, and after feeling the freedom of leaving my marriage, I didn't want to feel trapped again. Being content and showing my 'community' that I was happy didn't matter anymore; I needed more from life for myself, regardless of what they thought.

Promise yourself that you will not let anybody dictate your happiness. No one has control over what you allow happen to you except you. Tell yourself this. No one, absolutely no one can control *your* happiness. Every day is a learning curve and there will be days where you still think about past bad experiences (I've been there). But you must learn to be resilient. My coach Nadia Allam[1] gave me the best advice to overcome this:

"When you have days that are not good, think about all the obstacles that you have overcome, all the hardship – be proud because not a lot of people would have been able to survive what you have been through in life".

The key is, learn to **be proud** of everything you have overcome and remember you have overcome in the past and can do it again whether it's emotional abuse in marriage, disrespect in relationships, those days where you felt it was all over. The beauty of it all is that you survived. Bad phases come and go, whether they're long or short.

Resilience is a key word you must focus on; being able to overcome and get through a tough time without caving in. No matter what I went through in life and all the mess that followed, I survived. Here I am, writing about my life's journey, something I didn't think I'd be able to do.

There is no right or wrong answer, your journey has many routes and there will always be many solutions to a problem. You will only find out what works once you cross that road. No matter how bad and lonely the road may be at times, remind yourself that you have what it takes to not just survive but thrive. The truth is, no one will understand you better than you do; no one else will be able to understand you until you learn to care for and love yourself. Understand, support, learn

---

[1] https://corecultivator.com/

about, and nurture yourself. This might not come naturally to you, or happen overnight, but it happens with time and meaningful practice.

Believe me when I say this to you, true happiness comes from within. Of course, everyone is different; I have met so many friends, clients and acquaintances who have been through bad marriages and relationships and knew how to *'dodge the bullet.'* They realised quickly that their relationship just wasn't going to work. They were able to see the red flags and were able to save themselves. Some people are naturally like this, they have what it takes to leave without question because of their sense of self. Some of us must work on this with self-love. Loving self is very simple and yet so effective.

Learning to love yourself can only be done if you think about your emotions, and pay attention to how you think, and truly begin listening to you. One of the core foundations of NLP is to control your mind = control your life.

Tips on self-love and care

- Start a journal so you can explore your mind and feelings
- Have daily positive affirmations
- Go for a walk and start to love nature
- Listen to your gut
- Be patient

Journaling

I love to journal, whether it's a deeply personal stream of feelings or even little thoughts or ideas I have throughout the day, I would always write them in a notebook or my phone. But it didn't happen overnight. Believe me there were days I did not take any steps towards self-love and care. I would go days without brushing my hair. Real self-love and care are a work in progress. Yes, you heard me right, it is all about being consistent and making a commitment to yourself. I remember during the beginning of my personal transformational journey; I didn't want to work on myself. Everything just seemed such a chore, I would end up feeling drained, the whole thing seemed like such hard work. Even doing little things made me feel demotivated and disinterested in everyone and everything. But that is part of the journey, for without consistency and commitment you will not see any results. So, journaling is a good baby-step to take which you can build on little by little.

The most important thing is noting down your thoughts, feelings and whatever is going through your mind because it is a practical skill of self-care. What I really like about it is that you can write whatever you want, express yourself freely and feel safe. There's no judgement or bias from anyone. Try to journal when you're in private and have space, or if you find yourself alone, take advantage of that.

Positive Affirmations

Daily positive affirmations are so useful. I heard and have read of many benefits of positive affirmations. But it took me ages to grasp this concept, and really trying my hardest to practise affirmations. I think when you first introduce a new habit into your life, it naturally feels weird. Positive affirmations are positive statements that can help you overcome self-sabotage and negative thoughts. It will help you improve the perception you have of yourself and build your confidence.

Developing a strong sense of self-worth is what makes a person more likely to improve their inner self and mental wellbeing. If you start your day with five minutes of daily positive affirmations, the day will go much better and smoother. Some positive affirmations I like to tell myself are:

"I choose to be happy."

"I will be my best self."

"Only good things happen to me."

Nature – The Outdoors

Loving nature is such a wonderful feeling. Walking in the park, listening to birds chirping and winds rustling will wake you up. Doing daily exercise, like walking really helps your mental wellbeing. Even if you're not much of a walker, or don't feel like it, think of it as cleansing your mind rather than exercise. Whether you decide to go for a run, play sports, or practise yoga, any type of physical activity is essential for your personal wellbeing and development.

Your Gut

Your gut is such an interesting part of self you possess. First, your 'gut'; your instinct or intuition, will notice and feel things before you can properly see them yourself. Your gut will protect you, but how many of us listen or truly understand our gut feeling? Think about when you first met your toxic partner or someone toxic in your life, was your gut telling you something isn't right? Even once, did you have a feeling deep down inside that you knew there was something wrong? Some things don't always add up or make any sense. But you still go ahead ignoring it, which could result in catastrophic situations. This happened to me – I knew, deep down inside, something just wasn't right. Always listen to your instincts, they're usually right.

If you want to learn how to *dodge the bullet,* always listen to your instincts, especially if you can sense it is trying to show you red flags or something else you are unsure of. Please take the time to recognise and acknowledge these feelings. I'll be honest, I was never good at listening to my gut instincts – it took me quite some time to really understand or acknowledge what my guts were telling me and then evaluate my thoughts and process my feelings. It is a skill, and like every skill it takes practise to make it permanent. Next time you are feeling your gut instincts trying to tell you something, *listen, pause,* and *re-evaluate* the situation. Sometimes, when your mind is cluttered, clogged and overwhelmed with numerous thoughts, you miss red flags and what your gut is telling you. If you ignore the signs, you won't be able to *dodge any bullet.* Bullets hurt, so dodge them.

Be Patient

Finally, the last point - being patient. You've heard it many times and it's true: you should be patient with yourself when it comes to your personal growth. Give yourself the time to grow, heal and to build a relationship with self. Life is way too short, there's no point being hard on yourself. When you condemn self, you self-sabotage. Don't do that! You came to this earth for a purpose, so find your purpose in life, find your freedom and your strength – you will reach great heights where no one can hurt you and if they do, you will be able to bounce back quickly.

If people know they cannot touch or break you then that is when you'll be free to succeed and find life's purpose. And there may still be people who say negative things and try to bring you down, but it means nothing because **you love you**. Focus on your time now and focus on your personal growth. This is vital.

Allow me to add one more …

Confidence

I believe everyone is born with different sets of 'life skills' but sometimes, many of us do not know exactly how to use them to our advantage. You must use emotional intelligence, and that only comes from life experiences, learning and being a little ambitious. You see, you need to be ambitious in life, and I am not talking about your career here, I am talking about you as a person. If you don't have the drive to be better, or to do better than you will never succeed in your life's paths.

Having ambition and confidence in yourself is important. I remember this one time during my A-level Sociology class, Mr Rose, my teacher asked the class: What is the most important life skill people need? I remember my classmates were shouting various words, money, intelligence, and the list went on. Then Mr Rose said, 'Confidence.' Confidence is the most important thing in people's lives. It's more important than money, than intelligence, than anything else. I remember the whole class falling silent.

I think many of my classmates, including me weren't expecting that answer. Why would confidence be the most important thing in life? He explained, if you have confidence in yourself you can go to places, get that job, people will believe in you. If you are confident and have faith within yourself, you will see people will believe in you too. You need confidence in all aspects of life, even in your faith. You need to have confidence in the God you believe in, you need confidence in your values and the principles that you live by. You need confidence to believe and go on with your daily tasks and duties. You do what you do because you have the confidence to do all that you do. Even waking up in the morning, you need confidence, even going for that interview you need confidence. All aspects of life are circled around confidence. Without confidence your daily living would be difficult.

Over the years, that conversation with Mr Rose has made an impact on me. I thought about it for days, and as I grew older, understanding more and more, the meaning behind his wise words became clearer. I understand, yes, having confidence in everything that you believe in, every action that you take is the most important thing in life. Without confidence in faith, in relationships, in yourself, life would be so much harder. Every action has a purpose and meaning behind it. You need confidence to act. Confidence enables you to do things with care and affirmation. When you are confident in yourself, others will have confidence in you. It is a cycle that goes round and comes round. If you have confidence in the work that you do and endeavour, then only good things can come of it, because it is something that you have put your faith in, and positivity will shine through. For example, if you believe in a project and have 100% confidence in your work, then people will have faith in you also. Whereas, if you don't have confidence in your work or yourself than people will have less faith in you, because that is the message you are giving out to the world.

Now, let me share some thoughts on how to dodge the bullet.

Learning to Dodge the Bullet

Sometimes when you have so much around you, you tend to forget a lot of things. You get lost in all the noise and clutter that fill your mind. If you remain in this mess, you will continue in a cycle that causes you pain, and the most important person, that's **you**, will be left behind.

So, what does learn to *'dodge the bullet'* truly mean? It means learning to avoid a difficult situation (or person).

How you do this, is through the method of self-love already explored above and reading the signs, recognising and responding to red flags that may appear.

Red flags will always be here, being alert is necessary so you recognise them and stay safe. This is a special skill on its own and something you need to learn when making important decisions in life because many bad situations can be avoided.

Your life experiences will help you learn from it whether good or bad. I think there is good in every bad experience, because these experiences give you the opportunity to learn and mature and if you are ambitious, these experiences will help you remain determined, focused, and steady, encouraging you to prosper in the journey of life and your transformation from within will begin.

A LITTLE PART OF MY STORY

After I started to read 'self-help' and 'personal development' books, I began to implement some of the self-help care strategies. One of the first books that was given to me by my sister was *'You can heal your heart'* by Louise Hay. I started practising positive affirmations, I bought my first journal and since than I haven't stopped journaling. Not only did it help me de-stress and express my thoughts and emotions, but it also helped me get clearer perspectives and reflect on what is happening in the NOW; it also helped me think on my life experiences and gave me the opportunity to sift through the chaos that was going on around me.

What I did

I once heard someone say, "if you want to see any changes in your life, you first need to make that change a habit and remain consistent with it." This is very true! I am a living example; I purposely and consistently journaled as a ritual every day. There are days where I don't feel like writing anything, but I repeat what I wrote the previous day. The point of the matter is, you should stick to habits only then will you see the results you desire.

Why I began journaling and the first thing I wrote,

After being silenced so often, it felt liberating to write down my thoughts. I was free to express myself, no one could judge me, and no one else would know what was going on in my mind and heart. I remember the first few things I wrote about were the pain and anger I felt, I poured it all out. I felt a great sense of relief in doing this.

Going for walks and its effects on me

I started going for walks after my toxic marriage ended, although sometimes, I wish I did a lot of these things while I was still in the marriage. It would have helped me cope better. All the healing started after my divorce, the effect was immense, it gave me the chance to reflect, understand, and get to know me. Whereas before that, I was confused and all over the place. Self-healing helped me to re-evaluate my focus, and most importantly made me realise that I was being hard on myself.

How I started with affirmations and its effects on me

At first doing positive affirmations felt strange, it was all new to me, so I began listening to Podcasts and YouTube videos on positive affirmations. I listened to them every morning, even if it was for only 5 or 10 mins, I would listen and stay consistent with my routine. This is a must. After a long time, about 6 to 8 months, I started writing my own positive affirmations.

At the same time, I had hired a coach/therapist. During my sessions, I would go over some selfcare tools which I found quite useful. Although, when I started, I wasn't consistent, but I stuck to it until … this is important if you are serious about transformation. I was.

Which other way could I have handled the situation?

If I had to go through this again, I would listen to my gut instincts. I remember clearly, two weeks before the wedding, I felt like calling the wedding off; something inside me was telling me not to go ahead with this marriage. But I didn't listen to my guts. At that moment in time, I thought since the wedding cards had been printed, over 450 guests had been invited, I couldn't face it. Only now I think to myself, going through a cancelled wedding would have been so much easier than a divorce. But that is life, maybe there was a reason for me going through this. I can't change my past, but I can help others with their future.

"Well, if I had a do-over (we never do) but if I did, this is what I would do instead when it comes to dodging the bullet...this would be my advice...

Take your time, do not rush and make irrational decisions. If you are unsure about a man, seek advice from someone that you trust, could be a family member, friend, or someone whose opinions you trust just to get their impression. Someone told me recently, "If you have to second guess a decision, it's probably best not to go for it." When you decide, it should be crystal clear, it should feel good and natural, with no hesitation. This is very true, especially when it comes to decision-making about a man, women tend to over-think, and make excuses for their shortcomings. Do not do that unless you are willing to live with it.

A case study

Yes, someone that I know very well was engaged to a man for almost a year. This one time he lost his temper. This made her feel very upset, and she felt he had overstepped her boundaries. She thought that if he can lose his temper so early in the relationship, how would he act when they are married. She decided to call off the wedding.

CHAPTER TWO

INNER BLIPS AND GRIEF

"Praying has helped me the most when it
comes to dealing with inner blips and grief."

I have talked about self-care and the importance of it, I talked about dodging the bullet, by being mindful of red flags. I also talked about being in a toxic relationship and how this can negatively impact you and how to bounce back with hope and resilience.

When you start your transformational journey, you really must start digging deep and reflect on everything that you have been through. Whether you have been through inner childhood trauma, problems, or grief, it is important to be able to really dig deep and get to the bottom of these issues, because if you do not deal with them, trust me, they will come crawling back to haunt you. Part of your transformational journey is to heal self and learn how to rebuild you, starting from within. Women like you and I, have to learn how to be their own psychologist. Women like you and I have to learn life the hard way, have to learn how to be strong and stand up for ourselves. We have to learn how to take care of ourselves, rely and depend on learning how to get out of tough times.

No one will look out for you until you start to look out for yourself

So, in this chapter, I will talk about *'inner blips and grief.'* Everyone is different, some people straight away are aware of theirs and able to manage their inner issues quite significantly; and there are some people who may not be aware of their inner issues or do not know how to deal with it at all or even where to start. Regardless of where you are in life, whether you are self-aware or not, you need to deal with your inner issues. Sometimes self-acknowledgement, and self-acceptance is a start. No one was born perfect! Acknowledging you have issues is the first step for personal development and it is okay to take your time, rushing does you nor anyone else any good. The more time you take to self-heal, the better the results will be. Trust me on this! It took me many years before realising that I didn't deal with my childhood traumas, and it took me a long time to realise the impact it had in my life. I want you to take a few moments to dig deep and listen to your inner self. Is there anything that 'pops' into your mind that you didn't get the chance to deal with.

What are blips?

So, what are blips and what do you do about them? Life would have been just so much simpler if you did not have all these inner blips. Inner blips are there for a reason, but once you go through this book, you will re-discover yourself and find the true beautiful soul that you are. Before you get there, I want you to ask yourself, *"What are my inner blips?"*. Take a deep breath. Settle down with pen and paper, write out your thoughts; use words to create a mental picture. *"What is it that is taking over my emotions? Why do I feel so up and down?"*

Now, you and I can easily shift the blame on others or something else, but will that solve the problem? Will that answer all your questions. No, No and No! What you need to do is really connect with yourself and trust me, it is not easy; this is something that you cannot do overnight. Transformation is real work from within, takes time, and a lot of work. But once you pass this hurdle it will all be in the past, and believe me, it is a wonderful feeling, and you can finally breathe.

Once you begin using these tips on how to get rid of your inner blips below, which I have been using for a while now, you will notice that you are able to reflect on the issues that really bother you. I have been using these tips and benefitted immensely from it. Right now, at this exact moment, I have around seventeen problems, they range from health to finance, and from finance to personal dilemmas in life. But it's okay, it really is. I found the solutions to my problem and the end goal. I just need to work towards them one by one. I keep a note of it in my mobile. I like to have this tool handy, somewhere private with quick and safe access and where no one else can get to it.

Inner blips are to be solved not brushed away. Look at *inner blips* as 'unhealthy' and 'toxic' to both your mind and body. The sooner you eliminate them the better. Some blips can take longer to solve than others, but that's okay. Like they say, "Rome wasn't built in a day", neither were you. It took time for all your cells to formulate. There is no rush, you deal with your inner blips as well as you can, and whatever you do, please do your very best, nothing less. At least when you look back at your life, you can tell yourself you have done everything in your power to solve your problems. Whatever happens just happens! That is that. You cannot live a life of regret – happy today, sad tomorrow. For everything that happens in life there is always a reason and note - **you are in charge**. The problem is smaller than you, the problem is not bigger than you. So, you can fight whatever problems come your way. With the right tools and guidance, you can fully overcome your inner blips.

Below are tips on how to get rid of your inner blips:

- Take some time out to write down your problems.
- Take the time to reflect and look at your problems as something that is small and manageable.
- Take daily walks, write in your journal, and make daily affirmations.
- Take the time to learn about yourself and love you.
- Just be you, this is your life and only you are in control.

Dealing with grief

Some Psychologists say the terms used in grief, bereavement and mourning have many different meanings. Any type of loss means something has been taken away. Grief can be experienced in many ways, for example physically, mentally, and emotionally. Physical reactions could include stress related illnesses or physical problems. Mental illnesses may include stress, anger, sadness, and anxiety. Emotional and social reactions can include taking care of others or having financial responsibility for a household. Of course, these may vary depending on your situation, but the bottom line is, a person may go through many changes when there is a loss, and sometimes friends, family, or co-workers do not always understand the level of loss you may go through.

My Life Coach gave the best advice to deal with my grief and the importance of grieving: "grieving is not forgetting the pain or loss of a loved one, and grieving is **healing**." It enables you carry on with life and truly deal with the pain rather than carry the pain around with you every single day. The effect of grief can be enormous. If you are going through grief, whether it's a loss of a loved one or any other type of loss, for example, job, health, a young person, etc., please do speak with a therapist, or a friend. There are different stages to the grief process. It is important you recognise them. There are tons of books, and resources online that will help you to deal with grief.

If you do not overcome grief, you get stuck in a cycle of anger, pain, and despair. You may lose track of your inner self. It affects you emotionally and psychologically because you are consumed by grief, whether it's regarding a person or situation and is evidence that you haven't moved on. There will always be that feeling of despair hanging around you.

Nadia once gave me an exercise to do, she told me to write a letter to my beloved father. Honestly, it took me three months to pull myself together to write this letter to my father. Although, I knew he will never get to read it, I wanted to say my part. I never felt like I had the chance to say goodbye. The loss of my dad, for me as a child was sudden and I never had the chance to say my last words to him; one minute he was in the hospital and three days later he was gone. I was in shock. All I remember from that moment was the shock I felt and intense despair. I don't think I ever knew how to deal with my father's loss, even today, I am still grieving, that's what it feels like. BUT I think I am coping with it better, now that I am older. NOW, I pray about it more, whether it's during the morning, or at night, every time I think of him, I say a little prayer. Praying has helped me the most when it comes to dealing with inner blips and grief. This is something that I can do on my own time and anywhere.

Grief is a weight which if not resolved, is carried along everywhere you go impeding your life as weights do. It's best you deal with it and get it out of the way so you can move on with life. Do not carry that weight with you. Do not carry that sadness with you. All the time, you need to acknowledge your grief and sorrow, which is a natural reaction to loss. Grief can be caused by death or social loss, for example, divorce. This makes sense to me now; divorce is very painful. As I was going through my transformational journey, I came to realise that it is easier to deal with natural causes of grief such as the loss of a loved one, whereas with divorce, you end up having a strange relationship with yourself, almost like you end up blaming yourself, and you feel like it is your fault.

You deal with the latter so differently. In my culture, when there is a divorce, they tend to put the blame on someone, usually the woman. Only the person going through the divorce understands the loss and heartbreak and all that's involved.

I have seen many people use different strategies to cope with the loss of loved ones. There is no right or wrong way when it comes to dealing with loss, it is a journey of personal growth and healing. The only wrong way I would say is putting your life in danger or reacting in a way that does not build you no matter the pain you feel. Hurting yourself more than you already are does not heal.

Dealing with difficult times in your life makes you stronger and your coping ability depends on your mental health, religious or cultural background and more importantly, your support system. Research shows children whose parents have been through a divorce cope better when they have siblings, someone to share their experiences with; same goes with children who have come from an abusive family, they tend to console each other and deal with the situation better because they have each other. This may be because siblings help one another bounce back, creating a support system. Bereavement is the period after the loss when grief is experienced, and mourning occurs. Time spent in bereavement depends on how close or how attached you were to the person who died.

On the other hand, mourning is the period where people start to adapt to their loss. This could mean enacting cultural rituals, rules, and customs. For example, in the west you would wear black to a funeral ceremony, whereas in southeast India, Bangladesh and Pakistan you wear white as a sign of respect especially if you are the widow, you are expected to wear a white garment as a symbol of constant mourning for your husband. I remember when my father passed away, my mother changed into a white saree, and took all her jewellery off. She hasn't worn a piece of jewellery since then. I want to clarify that this is not a religious but cultural practise. In north and central India, a widow is compelled to adorn a white saree for the rest of her life after her husband has passed away.

For example, Orthodox Hinduism demands women renounce their earthly pleasures and live their days in worship. This is a 400-year-old Hindu tradition[2], where a woman is expected to leave her family and earthly pleasures behind. She is sent to an ashram (a religious centre) in Vrindavan, North Indian state of Uttar Pradesh also known as *the city of widows*, where women spend their lives observing pilgrims, going to temples and spend their time praying. These women are often ostracised

---

[2] https://qz.com/india/645988/indian-widows-colorfully-break-a-400-year-old-taboo-to-celebrate-the-festival-of-holi/

by the society and even their immediate family consider them as cursed. They believe if they live with the family members, it will bring bad luck to them so are often thrown out by their families. Not too long ago, on 21st March 2016, thousands of women gathered at temples in Vrindavan, to celebrate the festival of Holi (also known as the festival of colour) where Hindu's celebrate the season of spring. They violated their 400-year-old Hindu tradition, apparently it was not the first time. Some old traditions related to widows have been fading away in the urban cities in India, however, they are still strictly followed in the country's rural areas.

Can you imagine a woman in this position, not only did she lose her husband, but she is forced to leave her family, and children and spend the rest of her life alone, in an ashram with other women who have been violated and dehumanised? The fact that the loss of her husband had nothing to do with her and is not in her control is not considered, their culture is their reality. Seems like the people who are enforcing these rules and customs are in denial and delusional.

For me, this is heart-breaking; women being classified as zero class citizens in some communities. It is as if they have no status, no rights and have no say. It is known as 'social death' for women. Widows in these communities are generally in poverty and least protected by the law because their lives are determined by local, patriarchal interpretations of tradition, custom, and religion. Single women are perceived as property and under the control of their fathers, brothers, and their husbands. Widows are void, outcasts in society and no longer have any protector.

Although, it is not an easy thing to go through, unfortunately it is part of life and sooner or later we must all go through it. Dealing with our inner blips and griefs is an important part to being resilient and walking in your inner strength for transformation.

The main aim of dealing with grief is to be able to do it spiritually. To allow yourself the process of grieving by accepting the reality of the pain and loss. Sometimes, you can assume being spiritual protects you from hurt or grief. As time passes by, your emotions are less tense, and you heal. While grieving you need to give time to rebuild yourself.

You must allow yourself to process any type of grief, big or small. You need to give yourself time to heal. This is a very important step for your transformational journey.

MY STORY

A story about an inner blip I always had.

This is a tough one, but I will try my best.

I think when you start getting pitiful remarks either from your community or extended family, it becomes quite hard to deal with. I remember this one time, I think after a year my dad had passed away, a relative said, "Who will marry these girls with no father? In their eyes not having a father meant we weren't marriage material and they felt pity for us.

Perhaps it comes from patriarchal ideologies, where the father is the man of the house, the father makes all the decisions for the household. But for me, this wasn't the case any longer and I kept hearing these strange remarks from people.

What did I do?

I suppose, when you're young, you don't understand what's really going on, having said that, I always felt, just because I didn't have a father anymore, somehow, I was no longer accepted by the community that I was a part of. It felt like people gave us a hard time about it, I really disliked their 'pitiful' comments. If people make such remarks to my hearing now, I would give them a piece of my mind, but when you're young, you feel a bit helpless in these types of situations.

My thoughts on what I would have done differently

When I think back, it was a different 'era' then. If I could do this all over again, I would 'grow thicker skin' much earlier. I would be aware of my boundaries, and I would stand firm when someone crosses it.

What advice would I give myself today about inner blips?

Not to take it to the heart. People will always talk, they will always be mean, you just have to rise above it and not let anything bother you, life is too short for negativity. Live life to the fullest, and in the best way possible.

A case study

A client of mine had severe abandonment issues; her father left her as a young child, so growing up not having a father was tough. It affected her relationships, and personality. She had major trust issues not only with the men in her life, but with people in general.

She used to wonder why her relationships did not last. During my sessions with her we went through some tools on dealing with childhood traumas. They included recognizing the trauma, being patient with yourself and reflection.

Most people don't always understand or recognize that they may suffer from childhood trauma. It's always an oversight. But once you know what the problem is, there is always a way to deal with it. Being patient with yourself is also very important; self-criticism, fear of loneliness can trigger lots of anxiety in people's lives. I always tell my clients to be patient with themselves, often people blame themselves for what they went through, the main person that you need to re-assure is 'yourself', and that is a fact.

Finally, all this can be done through reflection, if you don't spend time and energy reflecting on past experiences and learning, you will limit yourself and close the door to a fulfilled life. I mentioned this before, it's not easy, that's why acknowledgement, being patient, and reflective with oneself is so powerful in self-development.

CHAPTER THREE

THE ART OF FORGIVENESS

"The freedom of finally letting go of the poison
that had been slowly eating me up on the inside,
is one of the best feelings I have ever had."

I t took me years to understand the concept of forgiveness. What is it really? And how easily can you forgive someone? Is it easier to say it, than to DO it? I think so! It takes a strong person to genuinely forgive someone. It took me a long time to forgive all the toxic people in my life. There are days when I think I have forgiven them and days when I think I have not. It is not because I didn't want to, but I just didn't not know how. I could not get myself to forgive for all the wrong doings. So many times, I have heard "forget" – "just forget and move on", but what I learnt is that is not always easy to do.

You are probably asking, what does forgiving have to do with **transformation**? Well let me tell you, it has everything to do with transformation. You see unforgiveness is a burden you carry in your heart and trust me the weight is heavy. The sooner you get rid of this burden, this nuisance, the freer you become. Transformation from within, is all about elevating yourself, being free from all the toxicity in your life.

For me I struggled with forgiving and moving on, I did not know how I could ever forgive those who had ruined my life. Well, I took the initiative, took charge, to learn and understand what forgiveness all is about.

Is forgiveness easy peasy?

Well forgiveness is easy, it is the forgetting that is the harder part and one day when you eventually forgive, you end up remembering the memories again and again, the spiral just continues. It is like a vicious cycle because, believe me, the work of forgiveness is one of the toughest jobs to do on oneself. I understood the beautiful **"art of forgiveness"**, when I found out **forgiveness sets you free from the burden of holding on to resentment and pain.** The freedom of finally letting go of the poison that had been slowly eating me up on the inside, is one of the best feelings I have ever had. I learnt about this feeling after reading about it, now I know why forgiveness is one of the things that uplifts your soul. It makes your spirit free; it enables you advance in life rather than carrying the burdens of unforgiveness. Forgiveness purifies and transforms you.

Forgiveness can help you find meaning in life's worst events and free you of the inner violence of your own rage. There are great myths about the concept of forgiveness. Some people may think forgiveness is a sign of weakness, by not standing up to those that do you wrong and are unkind. But this is not forgiveness. Forgiveness is not about letting others walk over you. Forgiveness is about how you hold your heart in times of terrible wrong, big or small.

The art of forgiveness is the practice of freeing your own emotions and finding meaning in the most terrible of life events. One thing that I have learnt is you do not 'forgive' for the sake of the other person; in fact, you forgive for '**yourself**' and only you. You do not forgive so that the other person is free from you, you forgive so that you can be free from them and let it all go so that you can heal and be the supreme being that you are.

Your Choice

You do have a choice. It's either you are 'wise' or 'wounded' from the experience that you had in your relationships. You must say to yourself, "Life is too short; too short to hold on to pain and drama."

That is what I did; I knew that to move forward, I would need to let go of all the negative memories, and feelings and quite simply, all the nonsense that I have been through. I was feeling overwhelmed with everything, that I did not even know the first basic step for how to forgive someone. So, I decided to take the matter into my own hands, and I thought to myself, it is **now or never.**

I first learnt about forgiveness when I was listening to a workshop by Mindvalley CEO Vishen Lakhiani[3]. He spoke about forgiveness, and it made me really question myself. *"Why do I have so much hate for this person? Why do I have bad feelings for this person?"* I used to pray for terrible things to happen to them, to be honest looking back now I am

---

[3] https://www.vishen.com/

not sure why I would speak or think in that way. I suppose it was my way of fighting back, I was tired of the thought that this person got away with the hurt and humiliation they caused me. I felt deeply hurt, and harbouring these vengeful thoughts and anger made me feel better but not for long, it only made me feel better for a moment or so. Yet, I held on to the toxic thoughts.

To tell you the truth, I became exhausted from carrying all the rage and anger within me until it got to the point that all I wanted was to get the weight of the burden off me. I grew tired of feeling hate towards this man and needed to figure a way out. A free way out where I did not have any hate, nor did I feel like a bad person. Although, I genuinely believed this man deserved all the bad things that could happen to him, he deserved it. But still, I did not want to feel like this towards him or any person any longer. I did not want to forgive because subconsciously I knew that on the day of judgement, he will have to answer to God for all the pain that he caused me, God forgives all, but he cannot forgive on behalf of someone. That made me feel comforted.

Looking back now, I realise that my thought process was **not** right, nor did it really sit well with me either. I was traumatised by these painful experiences and would say anything to myself that would make me feel and cope better.

There are studies[4] which have shown that just by forgiving others, there is a strong psychological benefit for the one who forgives. The study reports forgiveness reduces depression, anxiety, rage, and symptoms of PTSD (post-traumatic stress disorder). This was my light bulb moment. There was no point putting another second of my time

---

[4] https://greatergood.berkeley.edu/article/item/eight_keys_to_forgiveness

and energy into hating a man who did not deserve me in any way. Why should I allow him to win? By hating him, I was giving away my time and energy – myself - and he was winning. I did not want that, and that was the moment I decided that enough was enough, from now on I will not hold on to this rage and anger, and truly let go of all the hurt. It was not worth it then and it is not worth it now.

I transformed into a "hate-free woman."

The Process

Let us talk about the process now, although it did not happen with instantly. Forgiveness is a journey of its own. I think the first step for me was to learn about forgiveness. I knew that forgiveness is a key to high transformation but how does one get there? Really?

There is no right or wrong way of forgiving someone. I suppose this is just something that people must figure out.

Time is a healer, and it truly is. I do not think it is something that you can do hastily, it takes time - days, months, years who knows. **But the key is to really understand the relevance of forgiveness.** There is no pressure, there is no quick formula. Only you get to decide how the process of forgiveness should happen. It occurs over a period, and what's important is patience - be patient with yourself. The result will be well worth it, trust me. Forgiveness helps you to increase your self-esteem, your sense of strength and safety, it enables you to heal. Like I mentioned, it takes practice and patience. So don't give up once you begin your journey.

Most people are not aware, but there are two concepts of forgiveness:
True forgiveness

Half-hearted forgiveness

I spent half of my life forgiving half-heartedly but I realised this only after an exceptionally long time of self-reflection. Some of the people I had to forgive were those saying and doing me wrong, in a bid to make me stay in a marriage that was breaking me; even though they knew the relationship wasn't an ideal situation for me. I struggled to understand what they would gain from it.

I had women who would say to me, "You will die alone" or "it's uncommon for a divorced woman to re-marry in our culture. Think about how many divorced women you know that have re-married'?

I never believed in these statements; I resisted them because this was not the narrative I wanted in my life. Because they were untrue, in my culture and religion a woman can re-marry. I still found it hard to understand where they got their judgemental and narrow mindedness from.

Although, I didn't accept their statements, looking back now I think what hurt me the most was the fact that they were trying to make me feel small and this is something that I struggled to forgive them for. But I knew in my heart that I did not want to carry this burden in my life, and I knew that I needed to forgive them.

Leo Gura[5] founder of Actualized.org who specialises in self-help suggests that most people forgive half-heartedly and as a result, create even more toxicity in their relationships. Forgiveness is one of the most powerful tools for self-healing, and most people are unaware of how forgiving they must be in life. Forgiving people who have wronged you deeply is one of the hardest things anyone can do. However, I say this strictly from my experience.

_____

[5] https://www.actualized.org/leo-gura

However, can you truly forgive someone despite the pain they have caused you? It is important to break it down, have a set boundary in your relationship and ask yourself how and what exactly you will forgive.

How to set boundaries is a subject I will look at later in this book. I think setting boundaries in any relationship is about knowing and communicating what your values and standards are, no matter what sort of relationship it is.

Who to forgive or not?

There were obstacles right at the beginning of my marriage. I had to think twice whether I wanted to forgive or not. This was because I felt stuck in the relationship. I knew divorce was still a taboo in my culture, so I felt like I had no choice but to forgive in certain situations, because there were no other options. Although I felt a crazy rage and deep resentment towards him, there was no alternative but to forgive and forget the incident and move on. There was simply no escape at that moment in time, or so I thought.

Forgiveness was my only choice to remain in and continue the marriage. It was the only way to save it and I thought it would be the right thing to do in the circumstances. This required work, coupled with the ability and skills to do so. It was hard. People make forgiveness look like such an easy thing to do. For those who were perhaps born with the ability to forgive easily, it might be easy. But for the average Joe, it is not an easy thing to do. Especially when you are talking about spending the rest of your life with someone. You and I are humans, and humans make mistakes. How do you forgive the person that you will spend your life with? If you do not patch things up with your partner or an important person in your life, you could spend life watching your relationships end.

Let It Go

You know you can do ten good things to a person, but one bad turn and that is it, it can ruin the entire relationship. I have seen it with friends and family. You spend your life together, and you think you have a strong relationship with them. Then suddenly, one day, you realise that one silly mistake or a pointless argument can change the whole dynamic of the relationship. It makes you wonder at the fragility of human relationships. If you struggle to forgive a person you are not married to, no wonder it is much harder to forgive someone who is your spouse and has hurt you deeply.

Forgiveness is letting go and forgetting – there are two elements. If you do not let go, you are re-living the incident, constantly. It is like a scab on a wound. If you keep on picking at the scab, the wound will never heal. The same concept applies to forgiveness, if you keep on re-living and pondering on the bad moments, you are constantly picking at the hurt and pain. By picking at it, the pain will fester as time goes on. If you choose true forgiveness, then you can start by having a clean slate and not having to re-live the bad days. It is important to remember the past, but it should not stay with you, it only stays with you when you re-live them. That is why people find it challenging to let the past go. Be honest, if you do not quit blaming yourself for your past – forgiving another person is almost impossible. You must learn to truly forgive others and let your wrongs stay in the past so that your heart opens.

Without an open heart, this journey of forgiveness will be an empty road. The first person that you need to let off the hook is: **YOU**.

True forgiveness enables you to let go of everything. Interestingly, there is an element of self-righteousness when it comes to forgiveness. You can easily fall into a trap where you think you are 'better than them' just because you have forgiven them. It is important to be aware of this because it can be a problem. The purpose of forgiveness is not about being the better person but being the **bigger** person and to start from a clean slate by leaving the past behind, forgetting and moving on.

I spent so long reminiscing about the pain and hurt that I became a passive person. I think, on the outside, I was saying, "I forgive you" but on the inside I still had resentment. No matter what I tried, the feelings of negativity would remain. The truth is, the point of forgiveness is not about being half-hearted, rather, forgiveness is all about truly letting go of the pain that the person has caused you.

Decide

"Forget the wrong", that they did to you. This does mean you forgive every single person that has wronged you. The ultimate decision is yours, letting go and forgiveness is your choice. It is your life and only you have the right to decide whether you want to forgive or not.

Having said that, *you are not without feelings.* If your partner cheats, and is physically abusive, it is painful and may be harder to forgive them, and you do not have to feel guilty for not being able to forgive that person quickly. At the end of the day, that person has broken your trust and the covenant of your marriage. However, even though it may be harder for you to forgive, forgiveness frees you, remember this.

Although it could take a while to get to the place where you can forgive them so that you are free.

Everyone has a set of morals, values, and principles, and only you know how and when yours are crossed or/and broken. You can decide whether to reset the relationship boundary, or to just end it.

You do not realise that this is a decision that you make within, whether it is a conscious or subconscious decision. This process can only start by making a promise to yourself to forgive and let go of the pain the person has caused you and never to think about it again. This is a promise you make *within* you. The other person has nothing to do with it. To forgive someone sincerely, it takes strength and inner courage. Letting go is something that can start 'now,' not tomorrow or leaving it for another day. Promise yourself that you will not procrastinate, the journey of true forgiveness starts now and **from within.**

The Past ... It Is Toxic

Like I mentioned earlier, it is the forgetting part that is the hardest part. Your mind is like a sponge, it will absorb whatever you feed it, and if you keep on thinking of all the negativity and bad memories, the mind will keep on re-living and visualising all the wrong that was done, by living in the past.

What you need to do is keep track of the original promise that you made with yourself, don't forget that you made a promise that you will not go there anymore. Anytime your past's bad memories re-appear in your mind, be stern and remind yourself that you made a promise you will not entertain these thoughts anymore. It takes courage and strength for that to happen. If you are not willing to do this - have the strength and courage to choose thoughts that create a better future for you - you become vengeful; even though you have forgiven them, you still have thoughts of wanting to hurt them for what they did to you (like what I went through).

Vengeful forgiveness

"Vengeful forgiveness" is a type of forgiveness that is toxic to the soul. It will make you feel better for a moment, but eventually these vengeful feelings will build up until one day, you simply explode. As a result, your relationship will turn sour. The love you had for each other goes into a dark place and it becomes hard to turn back. All the resentment that you have will turn into negativity and toxicity. The creepy thing is this negative energy will start to affect other aspects of your life. You may not realise it, but the negative energy will start impacting your health, your mind, your career, and relationship with your family including other areas of your life.

Start **letting go** and **forgive**. You have the option to leave everything behind right now, but the question is: *do you want to?* Do you still want to hold on to the burden of rage inside you? Or truly start to forgive the people in your life that have deeply hurt you and letting go of the negativity that has been consuming your mind, body, and soul for so long.

You must decide right now. Whether the boundary that has been crossed is reparable or not. You might even be in a situation, where that person has disrespected your boundaries and you feel they cannot be truly forgiven by you. If that is the case, then you may not be able to forgive them now; move on with your life and work on forgiving them later but do not take too long. Decide, as quickly as you can, to forgive them and let the pain go. The sooner you can forgive and move into a new chapter in your life the better.

Maxwell Maltz in his book *Psycho-Cybernetics*[6], which really is not a book about forgiveness but mentions something interesting about 'forgiveness' wrote - *"true forgiveness is when you realise you have no reason to hate or judge the other person in the first place."* That is both a powerful and true statement. The truth is you might think you have reasons to hold onto this hate, but the fact of the matter is you own it to yourself. The way you think, the way your mind works. You are ultimately in charge. It is up to you how you condition your mind and pave the path of your heart. You are responsible for yourself, your happiness and how you transition from one stage to another.

Like I mentioned before, the problem with forgiveness is being stuck in the past. I was in that rat race for a very long time. I realised that holding on to negativity and feelings of revenge was an obstacle to my personal growth and spiritual development. I realised that by carrying this negative rage, it was blocking my dreams, and aspirations in life. I discovered my purpose; I realised that I wanted to achieve more in life and leave a legacy behind. I wanted to work towards my goals whether small or big. I wanted to achieve and reach personal fulfilment.

This negativity was quite frankly a pain to my whole being. I did not have the energy to carry this around with me anymore. I promised myself that I will not let my past traumas, sadness or anything that was tearing me apart put me down and win! I envisioned a future of me winning over trauma, changed my mind set and went onwards and upwards.

---

[6] Maltz M, (2015), *Psycho-Cybernetics,* Perigee Books

I was sick and tired of having limiting beliefs, I wanted to believe without limits, so I started to think big, dream big and work towards my goals day by day, learning how to transform my life as I went along.

The Journey

Do not get me wrong, there were days when I wanted to pull my hair out. Let us face it, life gets in the way, but it is good to remember, there is always a way out. Once you realise forgiveness is something that you need to do, then do it. Do not hang about. There is so much in life that is waiting for you. Whether that is meeting new people or making new friends, the chances, and opportunities are endless. The universe is too big to worry about petty and delusional people. It is not worth it at all. If you are feeling sorry for yourself, then no one can help you! You need to move forward with a momentum that will keep you connected and focused on your life's purpose.

A core solution is having a sense of mission in life. You will still have negative people who will wrong you in life, but you must not care too much because you will be too busy focusing on your life's purpose and goals. That is a beautiful place to be, being able to let go of negativity and forgive others easily.

Power of forgiveness

We have spoken about research that demonstrates the impact of forgiveness on your mind, body, and soul. I would like to explore this further.

Forgiveness is about you, and not the other person. When you forgive someone, you can feel the impact on you 'spiritually', as it enables you to have greater peace of mind. It helps you develop greater intuition. Forgiveness is about you - removing shame, guilt and other negative emotions that might be holding you back from being the supreme being that you are. The art of forgiveness is all about the manifestation of your intuition to reach the highest levels of spiritual wellbeing. Forgiveness allows you to be less reactive to criticism, judgement, and frustration.

There are great aspects of forgiveness, for example forgiveness is a subtle form of meditation. There is a great Dharma wisdom that says, *"Forgiveness is a spiritual practice"*, and it has been taught by many great Prophets and teachers.

Forgiveness is a gift you give yourself to be free of negative feelings and vengeful thoughts. Forgiveness, in other words, is fighting with your inner rage, set yourself free and liberate your own feelings. Rumi[7] says, *'forgiveness is the fragrance that flowers give when they are crushed'*. You cannot forgive until you have truly opened your heart and mind. Be open to inner transformation and self-love. When you hear about forgiveness, you have the tendency to think about forgiving others for the wrongs they have caused you. Whilst it is not easy to forgive others, letting go of past mistakes or misdeeds one has done can be harder. It is important to be able to forgive others for their mistakes, but also to let go of yours.

It is said, if you do not genuinely love yourself, you cannot genuinely love others, and this speaks volumes. You are taught to love yourself, but you are never taught to forgive yourself – maybe because loving

---

[7] https://www.rumi.org.uk/poetry/

yourself is way more important and vital. Because to forgive others, you must love them and we are unable to do unto others what we have not done unto ourselves rather, we are taught to be tough, and rough with self. Therefore, it is vital to love yourself. This is a crucial stage of transformation from within.

The weight of carrying the mistakes you have made throughout your lifetime is as heavy as a big rock. Reminding yourself that the world is not perfect, and neither are the people living in it will enable you recall that you also make mistakes which have consequences. Owning up to this does not mean you keep going around in circles beating yourself up about it. Just make amends where you need to and with whom you need to make them; and just as you need to forgive others for their wrongdoing, you also need to be forgiven. Take it easy. You are not God. He knows you will miss it here and there. Just do not stay there. Get up, dust yourself up and learn better so you can do better.

Dr Tyler VanderWeele[8], co-director of the Initiative on Health, Religion, and Spirituality at the Harvard T.H. Chan School of Public Health says: *"Forgiving a person who has wronged you is never easy but dwelling on those events and re-living them over and over can fill your mind with negative thoughts and suppressed anger, yet, when you learn to forgive, you are no longer trapped by the past actions of others and can finally feel free."*

I think it is that 're-living the experience' that is the obstacle in your mind that Dr VanderWeele is referring to. If you carry on remembering the bad experience, you are not helping yourself at all. He also suggests there are two sides to forgiveness, they are decisional and emotional.

---

[8] https://www.health.harvard.edu/mind-and-mood/the-power-of-forgiveness

Decisional & Emotional Forgiveness

Firstly, decisional forgiveness is when you choose to replace bad with good. You no longer desire to wish ill for that person or have vengeful thoughts. Apparently, this is much easier to accomplish.

Whereas emotional forgiveness is when you disassociate yourself from the negative feelings and no longer live in the past bad experience. This is much harder to do and can take longer to accomplish. Those feelings can return easily, this can happen when the memory is triggered, and you think about your offender. However, always remember that what you think about is your choice. You can change what you think just like that.

Observational studies show that forgiveness is linked to low levels of depression, anxiety, and hostility. Interestingly it increases higher self-esteem and better quality of life. Nevertheless, some of us had no idea about this. There is one simple way to practise small acts of forgiveness, and you can learn to do this in your day-to-day activities. For example, if someone jumps the queue whilst you are grocery shopping, take that moment to recognise that it was wrong of them to jump in and acknowledge that it wasn't aimed at you and forgive that person straight away. This is a great way to stop any negative feelings and reactions.

Forgiveness Meditation

Eastern philosophy is all about being compassionate, tender, kind and letting go of the harm or pain caused by someone else. They even practise silent meditation, where you just simply sit in silence for hours or even days without uttering a single word. They say silent meditation can benefit your relationship and those around you and most importantly helps to build a healthy relationship with **self**. It is scientifically proven that silent meditation helps you to gain effective concentration, but most importantly it improves your mind and body transformation.

For hundreds of years, meditation has helped people find their inner peace and harmony, although there are diverse types of meditation practices 'silent meditation' is the one that is most unique and hard to get used to, but once you do you will see the benefit it has on your spirituality. Especially when you are 'trying forgiveness' for the first time, silent meditation helps you focus on mindfulness of breathing and thoughts, feelings, and actions.

To begin with, you can start practicing silent meditation for ten minutes a day and gradually very slowly bringing it to thirty minutes to an hour. Morning works well for me, but it might be different for you. Whenever you want a moment to yourself, turn all distractions off and start meditating. The idea is to make a gradual start and staying consistent. Having a daily routine will help you and encourage you to stay focused on your meditation goals.

The purpose of meditation is to gain insight into the true nature of reality, not to let talking, noise or other forms of communication distract you. Meditation allows you to learn and accept things as they are and not how you expect them to be.

If you want to reach the higher level of transformation, it is important to seek forgiveness too. You are not perfect, by asking forgiveness from our mighty power, this opens the door of mercy and compassion. There are two kinds of forgiveness in Islam, they are God's forgiveness and human forgiveness. To be honest, you need both as no human is perfect and you will make mistakes. In Islamic teachings, we are taught to seek for forgiveness for any mistakes or sins against God and humans.

The Quran says, forgive others from your heart then God Almighty will give you the reward and you know God's rewards are best from all that exists. *"The reward of the evil is the evil thereof, but whosoever forgives and makes amends, his reward is upon God.*[9]*"*

If you start to think of forgiveness, and implement it in your life slowly, there awaits a greater reward. It helps you avoid negative thoughts, and grudges against others, and self-blame which are all toxins to the soul. Silent meditation, whether this means closing your eyes for a few minutes, helps you build that relationship with God and your inner self. It allows you to reflect deeply with contentment in your heart. It gives the opportunity to detach yourself from the world, from all the chaos and noise surrounding you. It helps you to connect with your mind and find inner peace in the journey of life. If you don't take the time to **reflect**, you are unaware of life; meditation gives you this awareness. It provides the opportunity for self-reflection and focus on the things that matter in your life. There will always be problems; it is just part of life. The act of forgiveness and acts of kindness are small steps that you can take to help you make things easier, getting rid of all the toxins and filling your heart with love and contentment. These are ways to achieve emotional clarity and calmness in life.

---

[9] Holy Quran, 42:40

My Story

It's an accumulation of events. Let's face it, you will always meet people who will hurt and disappoint you to your core. But that's life. The quicker you learn how to forgive people and move on, the better it is for you. What I have learnt is that forgiveness is one of those things that is inevitable, it is part of life. I have learnt this and still learning.

Have I forgiven those that hurt me? Absolutely. I can say this with hand on heart. Was it easy? No, of course it was not but I am in a better place in my life, and I wish them the best.

Time to move on. I am focused on my transformation journey, and I don't spend time thinking about the people who have hurt me.

What I did

TIME is a healer as they say, once I started to rebuild my life and career again, I honestly didn't have time to think about anyone or anything. I was totally focused on my purpose and life goals.

How did I forgive? But before that, how did I get to accept that I had to forgive? What was my process?

I took time out to think and had a deep conversation with MYSELF, what was it that I was angry about, what needed to be forgiven and what needed to be forgotten. Once I distinguished the two, I found it elevating to move on and start the forgiving process. I accepted that I needed to forgive, because I still felt rage, sadness, upset, and was emotionally distraught.

What is the beauty of forgiveness to me?

The beauty of forgiveness is that it sets you free. Because I've been through what I've been through, if I meet a friend or client going through a similar situation, I always tell them to start their 'forgiving journey' as quickly as they can. To get over someone, to move forward with your life, I think it starts with forgiveness.

Because all the negative energy coming from thinking of all the bad times, is what makes it' hard for us to move on with life. Therefore, forgiveness is important when it comes to inner transformation.

Did I engage in true or half-hearted forgiveness? If the latter, how did I overcome it?

I am not going to lie; it was a bit of both. Some days 'true forgiveness' other days 'half-hearted forgiveness;' but the truth of the matter is, it doesn't matter. The important thing is to note that you have started to forgive, for me it usually starts with half-hearted forgiveness, but later, as time passed and I matured in understanding the value of forgiving others, I would truly forgive. I am grateful to God that I got there because forgiving others is freeing yourself.

I overcame it by engaging in forgiveness. I knew I wasn't an 'expert' in forgiveness, but I had good intentions, and knew I wanted to transform and move on with my life, so I was happy to start taking the initial steps to forgiveness.

What did I let go off? What were the good and bad?

I had to let go of my pride or a better word, 'arrogance.' I can be stubborn, and forgiveness isn't easy for stubborn people, but I took the time for self-reflection. I knew my flaws, and I was eager to work on them. I didn't feel embarrassed to admit to my flaws, after all, it was to me not someone else.

For me, the BAD part was engaging in blaming myself for some of the things that happened to me. I had to learn how to forgive myself because I didn't know how. Being the stubborn woman that I was, I really had to dig deep to sort some of this out. Because I knew if I didn't, I wasn't going to help anyone, especially MYSELF.

Let me describe my forgiveness journey and tell you if I am still on it

100% I am still on my forgiveness journey. I don't think it ever stops, but you just learn how to be better at it. I think I mentioned earlier on in this chapter, that there were people I needed to forgive. Let's face it, misunderstandings, getting hurt is part of life, and that's why resilience is important because it teaches you how to deal with life's drama, complexities, and challenges.

Has the power of forgiveness helped me in any way?

The power of forgiveness has been a game changer. It set me free. I've learnt how to forgive; I've learnt how to let go of grudges and 'toxic' baggage around me. This wouldn't have been possible if it wasn't for the power of forgiveness.

It has given me confidence; I know in my heart I have good intentions, and that trivial things are irrelevant. I always try to look on the bright side, and I have become a better judge of situations and the consequences – I am better able to assess whether I allow someone to hurt me or not. I feel more in control of my emotions. I don't get upset easily, I am more open to giving people the benefit of doubt, however it doesn't mean that I let people walk over me.

I feel I am in a better place in life. A place where I am in control so that I respond rather than react emotionally to life's drama. And that's where I want others to be, in a good, strong place.

My advice if I had to do it again

Situations where I need to forgive someone is inevitable, that is life. If I had this time again, I would do what I do now and that is observe and assess situations first and choose to respond rather than react with uncontrolled emotion. I am better able to discipline my emotions, and less irrational (all over the place).

Here is some advice about forgiveness...

Relax, take a deep breath. Every process takes time. So have patience and believe that everything will fall in place in time.

A case study

I found meditation to be useful when it comes to forgiveness. The purpose of meditation is to gain insight on the true nature of reality, not to let talking, noise or other forms of communication distract you. Meditation allows us to learn and accept things as they are and not how you want them to be, it teaches patience; it will teach you how to listen to and relate with your thoughts and yourself more. Meditation teaches us to accept the world the way it is. It helps us to accept all the tragedies and hardships in life and helps us learn to cope with life's hardships.

CHAPTER FOUR

SETTING HEALTHY BOUNDARIES

"I think we are nurtured not to put our needs first, rather we are taught to put others needs first. That cycle needs to end."

S etting healthy boundaries, whether in a relationship, family or even professional setting is important. To be honest, I didn't really know much about setting healthy boundaries, like everything else in my life, I just didn't figure it out. It was in my first marriage that I realised the importance of setting boundaries. Like most aspects of my relationships, this is a skill that I had to learn and practise. It was incredibly challenging, but after some time I started to reap the benefits of setting boundaries. In any relationship, partners, co-workers, or family, being able to stand up for yourself is especially important. Otherwise, you will allow others to walk over you and invade your personal space. You cannot let that happen. But I think in a marriage setting, establishing healthy boundaries from the start is vital. You are probably asking, what does setting boundaries have to do with 'transformation?'. You see, there are different stages on the road to transformation, whatever the level.

The reason why I think setting boundaries is an important part of transformation is that I recognised that I didn't have boundaries and I allowed people to walk all over me. You can say I was being empathetic; empathy does not mean becoming a doormat. You need to have balance in life in the areas that you can because there are some areas you may never be able to create balance. Do not sweat over that, simply do what you can. I want to help you and make you realise the importance of setting down healthy boundaries in every area of your life.

Boundaries

I learnt that setting boundaries in a relationship creates good emotional health within a relationship. Boundaries are connected to our values and principles. They work side by side, yes, you just read "side by side." A boundary is a like a brick wall, until someone jumps over it uninvited. By crossing your stipulated boundary lines or jumping over your well-erected boundary walls, not only have you been disrespected, but you have also been taken advantage of.

Subconsciously, we all have "boundary walls," the only difference is some are obvious, and some are not. Over time, you keep the wall go up or lose your grip and let it down. Only you can control the height of your boundary wall. I do not think people know what their boundaries are. Be honest, have you ever asked yourself *'what the limitation of your boundary is?'* Can it change as time goes on? As we get older, our perspectives change, right?

This is not a conversation you can have over coffee with your friends, in fact if you tend to talk to friends when you have a problem, they will reveal their personal boundaries. Then you end up in a situation where you wonder, what is my boundary?

As you go along the journey of life in self-reflection and self-care, you must identify what your boundaries are, and make them clear. Setting boundaries helps you and not the other person. The other person will not benefit from a boundary. Mark Manson[10] mentions, *"healthy personal boundaries equal taking responsibility for your own actions and emotions, while not taking responsibility for the actions or emotions of others"*. Let me repeat that: *"healthy personal boundaries equal taking responsibility for your own actions and emotions, while not taking responsibility for the actions or emotions of others"*.

This echoes that you are responsible for your own way of thinking and feeling. You are responsible, and you need to own up for your actions and emotions.

To maintain both physical and emotional health, setting boundaries is essential. It is empowering for a person to create healthy boundaries; by establishing and implementing limits, a person can protect their self-esteem and self-respect, which are key for healthy relationships. If there is an unhealthy boundary in a relationship this can cause resentment, depression, and stress-related illnesses all of which, quite frankly, you need to avoid. By not having boundaries, you are leaving the door open, and people will enter or exit as they wish. This is particularly **not** healthy for you. I cannot stress enough, the importance of setting boundaries.

My advice would be to challenge any misbehaviour straight away, if you do not like a way a person talks to you, find a suitable moment, and talk things over in a calm, respectful and dignified manner. It is not

---

[10] https://markmanson.net/boundaries

about what **you** say that counts, but **how** you say things that matter. It is all about your communication style. As I have evolved and transformed as a person, I realise that setting boundaries was one of the most important steps I took that helped me pave the way.

Communication

Effective communication in a relationship is, I believe, what makes or breaks a relationship. It is what makes it work and keeps it strong or what destroys it.

I struggled with communication throughout my life, and there are days when I still think I haven't got it right but do we not all experience one form of weakness or another in character? Communication is a learnt skill, and on reflection, it is not a skill that I grew up learning. I always found it difficult to express my thoughts and feelings. I was always the one that repressed herself, while letting the other person talk, expressing their point of view especially in a relationship setting. Just to avoid confrontation and an argument, I would let things pass - "sweep them under the carpet." This is not the best way, because I found that by not expressing myself, I inevitably held onto pain and feelings of repression. When I look back now, that was not the healthiest thing to do. Unfortunately, some unhealthy habits never seem to die, I do occasionally *"go along, to get along."* However, having good communications skills is one way to manage boundaries.

Dr Ramani[11] spoke about this in her work on 'Narcissism' and why setting healthy boundaries is an important part of any relationship, whether that be romantic, professional, or even a friendship relationship.

---

[11] https://doctor-ramani.com/

However, if you are in a relationship with a narcissist, setting boundaries is even more crucial. One of the main reasons why people are afraid of setting boundaries is because they worry about how the other person may feel or react. Sometimes, it may be due to confidence issues. Dr Ramani talks about this 'fear' and how philosophers such as Lao Tzu have a saying, *"if you care what other people think, and you will forever be a prisoner."*

3 Possible Reactions to People With Toxic Energy

The interesting thing is when you are in an argument with a toxic person, three things happen. Either (1) fight, (2) flight (flee) or (3) freeze.

The "3 F's" as I call them, you have probably heard of these terms before. You have 3 options you either fight, flee, or freeze. I can relate to #3, as I recall every time I was in an argument - I would freeze, something like you have never seen before. Like I would just sit and stare "shocked" from all the absurd things I would hear and see. I would think to myself, what normal human being would do or say things like this? I was experiencing a flabbergast. It was like living a nightmare, a nightmare that you never wake up from. The intense toxicity was eating me up inside to the point I could not take it anymore.

When you try to set a boundary with a person with toxic energy, you may fail on the first attempt, and you might even feel guilty for trying at all. Guilty, may be because that person is making you feel that way or rather, because you do not have the wisdom to stand up to them yet and be strong. When you are in that situation, it is extremely easy to give in just to get along. You end up completely disregarding the boundaries that you initially set up. So, how do you establish strong boundaries? Where do you begin?

How to Set Strong Boundaries

Quite simply, there is no right or wrong way. How you set a boundary totally depends on your relationship. I remember when I first tried to put my foot down, I was in fear. I was fearful of his reaction; I would be thinking about how he would respond. What will he do? I started questioning myself. It was intense work I did not know I did not need to do; I began to feel like an analyst.

You need to figure out what the best course of action is and commit to your decisions. For example, if someone has said unkind words to you, you need to tell them that you will not talk to them if they continue speaking to you in that manner, and if they do, you will walk away from them. This will let them know that you are serious and authoritative. But you will have to find the courage to stand your ground. I know, I know it is easier said than done, but you must try. If it does not work the first time, you can try again the second time.

I have been there. In my community, women aren't expected to be heard. They are seen as second-class citizens in the household where men run the show and women are seen as doormats who just sit and stare. I know that feeling. The feeling of a man invading your space and disrespecting you. It is so difficult to set boundaries with a person with toxic energy. No matter how much you try, you may not get the result you want.

At first, in the marriage, I found it tough, very tough. Especially when you marry a stranger, and move in with them on the wedding night, move in with their family; this person with a different upbringing to yours; you don't know each other at all. Settling in and pretending to be a happy couple is exhausting. Eventually, the cracks begin to show. My only regret is I wished I had a set of boundaries before I stepped into the marriage. Knowing and understanding yourself is the key to setting healthy boundaries. I don't want women from my community to face that, ever. It's not a nice feeling. Otherwise, you will spend your life with people walking over you like they do a carpet without regard for you, for the rest of your life!

You must learn how to cope with uncomfortable situations. You must prepare yourself for the worst but stand your ground. Always.

Reality Check

It's interesting that when I started writing this chapter on setting boundaries, I thought a boundary was all about the other person, but in reality, it is all about you, but the '**you**' that holds up to, values and understands boundaries. Setting boundaries is about the relationship you have with your self and the values and principles you live by. Ask questions. Question everything that is not in alignment with your values or that you are uncomfortable with. There is nothing wrong with asking questions. Believe me, that is how you get answers and clarity. I see it everyday, young muslim girls step into marriages without putting much thought into what a marriage is all about. They are absolutely clueless. They have no idea at all. Marriage isn't like Bollywood movies, with the man sweeping you off your feet. No. There were times in my life where I didn't take a stand. If you don't take a stand and make it clear, don't expect a man to know what your standards are. You need to show him.

Another thing I found is that no boundaries equals low self-esteem. It took me a while to accept this bold statement but in reality, it is true. If you think about it logically, the reasons why you do not have a boundary is because you have low self-esteem. You don't believe in your own values and you do not believe you are a person of value, a person of worth. Bottom line is, if you don't believe in your principles or values, don't expect someone else to respect your boundaries. I think the problem is most people don't know what their boundaries are, whereas it should flow naturally off your tongue and with ease. The first step is to do a reality check and ask, *"What are my boundaries?"* *"What am I willing to brush off or accept?"*.

You need to repeat this exercise, until you get it right. Digging deep will help you recognise what your values are and instead of focusing on how to set boundaries for the other person, try setting boundaries for yourself. Understand, and ask yourself 'why?' Why are you doing this and going through that? For example, not once but there were many times I didn't express my inner thoughts. Probably out of fear, or maybe I was worried about his reaction. I wasn't myself. I didn't want him to judge me, because feeling judged is awful. It took a long time to realise that I was being gaslighted and if it wasn't for all the books I read and for the fact that I was on my journey of personal development transformation, I wouldn't have known what had happened to me.

The work on personal growth connects with self esteem, they both play a part. You need to work on your inner self first before concentrating on others. My best friends Dad always says, *"you can't teach an old dog new tricks."* Put simply, people (may) never change and you can never change anyone. The only way a person can change is if they actually change themselves. People are responsible for themselves for their actions and for their words. You can be responsible only for you, your actions, words and thoughts. You are better off concentrating on yourself and how you want to live your life and be the person that you aspire to be.

Boundaries honour your needs and values, not those of the other person. Part of the reality check as you go deeper, is to write in your **journal** a reminder for you of what your boundaries are. Actions speak louder than words, let your actions dictate, not your words. People will always try to push your buttons but that's okay, they will try their best to disrespect you, that too is okay. What is not okay is if you accept the disrespect and the disregard of your boundaries. The only way you will know that this kind of behaviour does not affect you is when you do not have an emotional reaction to the situation. Your boundaries are your core value and when someone becomes aware of your boundaries, they will test you.

One of the key components of boundaries is how passionately you express them. The more you value your boundaries, the better your communication. You are what you say you are, if you act on your values every single day, you are bound to live by the principles you believe. In Stephen Covey's book *'The 7 Habits of Highly Effective People[12]'*, he writes about living life with principles, dignity, and fairness. Part of being fair is being fair with yourself, you have to be fair to yourself. It is easy to judge the other person. But the truth is, if you don't respect your own boundaries, then how can you expect someone else to do so? The most important person that you should be kind to is yourself, and even that is rarely consistently done.

By having regular check ups with yourself you can really connect **within**. It's important to have that 'me time', whether that's for five, ten

---

[12] Covey, S. (2020); *The 7 habits of effective people*; Simon & Schuster

or thirty minutes, having a short break in the middle of the day not only gives you a chance to reflect but also to connect with your mind and helps you relax. Just by taking a few deep breaths can **transform** how you feel for the rest of the day. If you consistently maintain this reflective exercise, you will benefit greatly.

As you become more mindful of yourself, you will become more confident with an increase in self-esteem. Once you grow your self-esteem, setting boundaries will be a 'piece of cake.' You won't even notice how you naturally set boundaries, it is a process and does need some mindful work. But once you get a hang of it, everything else will fall naturaly into place.

Just remember, you are **setting the boundary** for yourself not for the other person. You can only do this if you are confident in yourself, your values, and most importantly your principles. Having boundaries reaffirms this and will show the other person what you stand for. The *'reality check'* exercises will enable you to do this, it will enable you see and analyse how important having boundaries is. Boundaries do not only keep bad relationships out, but it also helps to keep good relationships.

Dr Henry Cloud and Dr John Townsend mention in their book *'Boundaries*[13]' that one sign of having no boundaries is when one person has the power to adversely affect a relationhip; it means you are giving one person way too much power in your life. I think when it comes to being in a toxic relationship, this is very common, it's like the other person terrorises you by injecting themselves into your thoughts. You become aggitated, and you can not relax when you are with other people. You seem always stressed because they are on your mind

---

[13] Cloud.H & Townsend. J, (2017), *Boundaries*, Zondervan
https://en.wikipedia.org/wiki/Gaslighting

hoping they do not do or say something that will add to the stress. This can be because you have not put boundaries in place or your boundaries are constantly being ignored and you have not addressed it. It puts you in a position where you are not in control.

Boundaries help us to take a **resilient** approach to life. It helps us to protect ourselves, and helps us behave in ways that ensure we keep safe. Putting yourself first is always important, which in reality you and I do not always do. This is where self-care comes into play.

By setting boundaries in your personal life, you are able to take care of yourself, you are telling your mind that you matter. Boundaries protect, and keep you safe when things go wrong in life as it would normally.

There will always be trials and tribulations in our lives. When you become clearer about how you make decisions, and how you set boundaries with others, knowing when to say 'No,' when something doesn't align with your way. Ultimately, it is all about how people align with you, whether they cross the line or not and if they do, how how you respond, the impact on them and '*how it makes you feel?*'

When something does not feel right, your gut will tell you and you will 'just know.' This happens often when someone oversteps your boundaries.

In order to set boundaries, it is important to recognise your feelings first. It's not about the impact your boundaries will have on the other person. You must differentiate the two. Now, whether you set boundaries in a relationship or with a friend, being in touch with your feelings is how you recognise how to set the boundaries you wish.

My story

What were my boundaryless days like? What was my first realisation?

When I found I was afraid to voice my opinion, or to say anything just to avoid any type of reaction, that's when I knew I had no boundaries. On numerous occasions I would feel people have stepped over the line, but I felt helpless, that's when I realised that I needed to do something, and that I needed to set boundaries in my life.

What I did and some advice

Not so much with my ex, but with my husband now, I feel I have a better way of setting boundaries. I found that 'dictating' my boundaries did not work. Instead, I focused on my tone of voice because I have learnt that with men, it's all about how you say it, so rather than saying *you did this or you did that,'* say *'we need to look into this,'* or *'let's have a chat.'*

If you jump on a man and start naming and blaming, the dynamics of that conversation is wrong from the onset. Instead, take a calmer approach, but still being firm with your message. If you see your man isn't in a good mood, it's okay, choose a later time when he will be more inclined to listen to you. Assess the person first before you set any type of boundaries, because you want your boundaries to be heard, understood and respected. If you throw them at him like a brick, he will not 'hear' you and your boundaries will remain yours, without any buy-in from him.

What I would do differently if I could go back in time

Gosh! I don't really want that time back! But I would have taken a different approach, be a bit smarter about it, whereas before, I was just so emotional and would say things from the heart without control. Some argue that you should speak from the head, I do not agree, you should speak from the heart with control because the heart is who you are and how you feel – the authentic 'YOU.' The head is distant and should be used alongside the heart but with moderation and wisdom.

As a woman, you need to stay focussed, and be on guard. By being on guard, I do not mean you should expect your husband to overstep your boundaries, but that you should be self-aware enough to know you are not allowing yourself be led by uncontrolled emotions. Therefore, emotional intelligence is vital. Some women may not agree with me, but that's reality. You give a man one step, they will take 10 steps. Not because they are bad people, but because men are wired to lead and are not wired as we are, with intuition, however, you can help him by gently pointing out what helps you thrive. Do it. Do not be afraid. It will help your relationship ultimately.

If you know what you want from the relationship (any relationship) you need to set boundaries. Otherwise, people will dishonour you; however, do it nicely. Have good intention, and a clean heart and it will go well.

What advice would I give myself now? What would I tell me to do instead?

Trust my instinct, trust the process, and believe in myself that I can do it.

At first, setting boundaries is hard, especially when you don't have a clue, and I think it goes a lot deeper than that. I think we are nurtured not to put our needs first, rather we are taught to put others needs first. That cycle needs to end, I tried and still am continually trying to break the cycle. It's not easy but being overly empathetic is not right. Be empathetic but not over the top. I am learning to observe more and think a bit deeper before I speak. I have more self-control and confidence than I did before.

A case study

'Sleeping with the enemy' – I remember watching this movie when I was young, not thinking too much about it apart from the fact that it is a good movie. It was only after I got married, that I was really able to resonate with Julia Roberts. If you haven't watched this movie - spoiler alert - it's about a woman who fakes her death to get away from her controlling and abusive husband.

Of course, this is an extreme case scenario, but being in a controlling relationship is stifling; you feel so helpless, and vulnarable. One thing I've learnt over the years, you have to take responsibility for how someone treats you, espcially at the start of a relationship. So ladies, if you are currently courting (or getting to know someone), look out for the red flags, like any controlling behaviour. Set your boundaries NOW, don't wait till you get a ring on that finger, because trust me, it will be too late – although, it is never late.

From the start of any relationship, set your boundaries, make it clear. If a man sticks around than he is a keeper. It shows he respects you enough to abide by your boundaries. However, if he runs a mile, than you know he is not worthy of you.

CHAPTER FIVE

RESILIENCE IS EXCELLENCE

> "As much as you would like to live in a safety
> net or bubble, the reality is you will have to
> come out of this safety net one day to rebuild your
> life regardless of what the circumstances are."

R esilience is something you can learn, because being resilient is learnt behaviour. But what does it mean to be resilient?

Try to imagine **resilience** as a tree being buffeted by strong winds. The wind blows, the tree bends and bounces back to its centre. Resilience has the same concept; it is when life throws challenges at you, and you **bounce** back. The concept sounds quite simple, but bouncing back is one of the toughest things you can do. If at any point in life bouncing back has been challenging, I will tell you how you can come out of it stronger. Learning how to come to terms with the whole experience and learning to bounce back when the situation seems impossible is gold.

Resilience is something that is for all ages and not a specific behaviour that is repeated the same way each time. It varies depending on the situation you find yourself. This is something that should be taught to children from an early age, getting them ready for the real world. I strongly believe this.

You live in a world where there are constant setbacks, and difficulties and sometimes you are not ready for the real world, you will need to develop the ability to be resilient in such a world. As much as you would like to live in a safety net or bubble, the reality is you will have to come out of this safety net one day to rebuild your life regardless of what the circumstances are.

Resilience is one of those attributes in life that make you realise how **strong** you are. This all goes back to reflection; it is through reflecting on past events and situations that make you realise how powerful you are. You build strength by learning from the past. What happened? What can I do better? What did I learn from it?

To begin the journey of transformational resilience, you must dig deep again. Did anything happen in your childhood that impacted you? If so, how did you bounce back?

I searched within me, and I looked deeply. There were times that I did not deal with an incident, I quite simply would block it out. Looking back now, I always managed to go past the hurdles on my way. Come to think of it now, 'resilience' is what helped me go through those horrible experiences.

Let's face it, being a divorcee today is still taboo in my community. It's still such a problem but why? I'll tell you why. Because men run the show. It's the men who think women are at the bottom of the pyramid. If you are married, you get accepted into the community. The funny thing is, who wants to be part of this community anyway? No one is there for you when you need help. The community isn't there for you, paying your bills and putting food on your table. You are on your own, left to face your difficulties even if you don't know what to do.

I consider myself lucky that I live in a country where I can work and rely on me. How about all the women who live back home where they can't work and be financially independent? It makes such a difference in life just to have that little bit of independence.

Resilience is a blessing not a burden

Resilience is a blessing in disguise, although when you are going through a difficult time, you just want the whole thing to be over, but resilience is what educates you to be patient, it teaches you the ropes on how to stay firm and strong and that you can overcome anything that comes your way. Being resilient does not mean that you do not experience trauma or stress, in fact it is quite the opposite. Being resilient means, you can still face the emotions that stress and trauma cause, and you are better able to deal with hardships that come your way.

People who have high resilience can find the positive aspect in any situation; they are good at finding and learning from the lessons in negative experiences so they can apply it in future situations. In all honesty, there were times where having high levels of resilience felt like a burden to me.

I remember this one time; I was about 10 years old, vacationing in Bangladesh. My father and I were in a 'tuk tuk' on our way to the train station extremely excited that we were going to my cousin's wedding. In Dhaka, Bangladesh the streets are chaotic, no zebra crossings on the streets unlike here in the UK. Our tuk tuk driver almost hit this lady, so to avoid hitting her, the driver turned away and collided with another vehicle. Our vehicle was upside down, leaving my father and I with injuries. For a second, I thought someone had died. Unfortunately for me, my father had his first mild stroke due to the accident. He never recovered from it, and three months later his heart deteriorated, and he passed away. As a child, when you experience something like this it creates deep sadness in your life. I was angry at the 'tuk tuk' driver, I was angry at the lady for crossing the road recklessly. Everything happened so quickly, it felt like it didn't fully register in my mind. The whole time the experience felt strange. I was trying my best to process it all, the grief, the loss, the shock, the hurt, the anger. As a little girl, you can imagine how confusing and difficult that was.

Back in those days, getting help for mental-health was not a popular thing. These days there is awareness, and you can get help for young children. I grew up in a community where you didn't talk about these things. You just continue as if nothing has happened. That is how I learnt to deal with things as a child. Looking back now, these were pivotal experiences that shaped my life and taught me the essential skills to develop **resilience**. But it is not easy; as a child I would block out my emotions. I always felt I could not express my emotions, because no one would listen. It became a burden in my life. As I grew older, I had to change this narrative, because I noticed it had adverse effects on me, my friendships and relationships both at work and outside work.

Coming to a realisation

One thing I did grasp is no one is going out there looking for trauma, it happens. What and how you learn from these experiences is up to you, resilience is what keeps you going, every time you fall. It enables you fight through the tough times with courage and discipline and this can be any type of experience, big or small. Everyone has problems no matter where or who you are, it is how you manage your problems that will change your life. Many psychologists describe resilience as the process of adapting well in the face of adversity, trauma, tragedy, threats, or outstanding sources of stress for example family, relationship problems, health, workplace and or financial issues. One thing I realised that some psychologists do not describe is during the process of adapting to adversity, there is a moment where your whole life's adversity just reappears in front of your eyes in one go. What I mean by this is, during the process past emotions sometimes get triggered. If this happens to you, try to remember rather than sulking over it, that this is the moment to forgive yourself for what happened in the past. The past is gone, there is nothing you can do to go back, rather than focusing on what happened because it will not help but hurt you. It is best not to let anything trigger you. If it does, deal with it, by acknowledging the issue.

Many times, you probably *put it under the blanket* and not deal with what is really going on in your life. If you block everything, like I did with my childhood trauma, it will not help you move on. You need positivity and joy in your life so deal with it or it will only set you back, and that is not a place you want to be, never give in to an excuse or reason to fall back. Rather bounce back again and again, you must remember you have the power to **'make things happen'** in your life.

Problems happen in life

Resilience will only put you forward in life. Problems will always come and go, like I mentioned before, it is how you deal with your problems that count.

Only you get to decide which direction to go, no one else. You can spend your life sulking or learning how to be resilient and facing your inner demons. There is no right or wrong answer, it is your choice! No one can help you unless you help yourself.

That is what this book is all about, it is about being mindful of your life. Tools that can help you to transform your life, and make you realise that whatever life throws at you, you will be able to handle and manage life in a way that will make you happy. Becoming resilient is not a day's job but rather a skill that can be developed and practiced over time.

There was this one time, I had been trying for a promotion for a while. I went for interviews but did not get the promotion I wanted. I did not understand why; I did all the work, I practiced, I did all the necessary research – but nothing. It was getting me down. I decided to pull myself together and had a deep conversation with myself. I asked myself *'why did I want this promotion'* - *is it because of money, did I want a change, what is it that I want?'* After deep reflection, I realised I wanted a change. The universe is always right, it will give you what you want. You just must ask at the right time. The universe didn't want me to progress through the route that I wanted, rather I had a gut feeling that I should follow my passion and really pursue the career that I will enjoy.

You see sometimes you jump and go for things that you think might help or things that you need. You want things that you learnt from social upbringing, culture, or religion. I did not need the promotion but pursued a career that I had a passion for. I realised that I was rushing into making a decision; once I understood this, I took a step back and made a conscious decision not to stress or worry about it. Instead, I focused on myself, I prayed, I took a positive approach towards my career, I shifted my mindset. I think you might guess what happened next, things started to look up for me. I started to get more opportunities and projects that I had a passion for. Not just at work, but with my personal life too. Out of the blue, a friend of mine approached me to give a coaching session to some of her clients. This just goes to show, sometimes in life if one door closes another door opens. That is the beauty of resilience. It is your attitude towards problems that counts the most, you can either react or respond and be in **control** of your **actions**. You will block opportunities in life, if you do not continue to pick yourself up when you fall.

Remember everyone falls, but everyone can rise too. It is in challenging times when you need this skill the most. It is at such moments that you need to believe in yourself, stay strong and stay focused on what you believe in. This consistency is what makes resilience most excellent. It enables you to reach the transformational stage that you need to get to.

When I first started to write this chapter, I wondered what the best way will be to approach this. Do I just talk about how I survived all my life through resilience and perseverance, or do I just talk about my journey of learning resilience? There were times, when I realised how difficult some parts of my life were, but I overcame it somehow. It is through these toughest times, that I knew how strong I was and how effectively I dealt with my problems.

I am proud, blessed and quite frankly glad that those chapters of my life are over. When I look back now, I wonder how I overcame those moments - depression, low self-esteem, feeling like I have been through so much. I always remind myself that *'life goes on, and people move on and so must you.'* The days where I felt I couldn't go any further; the days where I wanted to sit in silence and wonder where the hell my life is going. Those are the days that I am about. The days that you mentally block yourself out.

Nowadays, those problems just do not seem that big a deal anymore, because I fought with won those challenges, started to rebuild my life, and at the end of the day, life is what it is and what you make of it. You and I are all new to this, and there is no right or wrong answer, and no one knows exactly what they are doing. You find a way, and it comes to you. You must find how to master resilience along with all the other things that I have talked about so far to help you reach your transformational goals.

Just enjoy the moment, mastering resilience will only help you along the way.

We know how important resilience is, yet many of us spend extraordinarily little time integrating it into our daily lives. It is the main foundation of successful people, and successful companies, when people come back stronger after a disappointment in life. Coming back stronger and more determined is the name of life's game.

There are tons and tons of research that have been published regarding the benefit of being resilient. According to Mayo Clinic[14], the most valuable tool for improving our resilience is to train our awareness and attention. Once you master resilience you can deal with life's problems in a rational way. It enables you to spend less time on things that do not deserve your attention. It is the power of resilience that enables you to do that by developing a sense of control and believing in yourself. An important thing to note is not to let all the chaos in your world affect you.

Believing that things will work out in life, Dr Lucy Hone[15] a resilience expert and Director of the New Zealand - Institute of Wellbeing & Resilience, shares her three strategies that helped her go through her

---

[14] https://positivepsychology.com/resilience-training-build-resilient-individuals-groups/

[15] Hone, L. (2017), *Resilient Grieving; Finding Strength and Embracing Life After a Loss That Changes Everything*; The Experiment; 1st edition

tragedies. After losing her young daughter and going through unimaginable pain she gives us insight on human suffering, and the impact it has on our mental health. The main thing Dr Hone talks about is that life's problems are not personal and the mere fact that tragic things happen is just part of life. The sooner you can accept this reality, the sooner you are able to cope with traumatic life experiences and starting your life again.

We spend a lot of time not accepting reality, when life brings us obstacles and challenges. When life hits us hard, you cannot take the pain and you end up feeling like it is just you going through this. What I like about Lucy's tools is that it is basic and simple that you forget to think yes, suffering is part of this life. Unfortunately, bad things happen, and it is not in our control. The only thing you have control over is how you react to the situation. The only way you can do this is by being kind to yourself.

Steps to resilience

Gratitude is such an essential element of resilience. Being grateful at times when you are at your lowest point is most powerful, but so hard to do. I am always conscious of being grateful. I think, sometimes, especially during tough times, we forget about our blessings and all the things that we should be grateful for. For me, keeping a gratitude journal has psychologically reminded me of all the greatness that I had in life. Even if you do not get to write it down, try to think about three things that you are grateful for every day, or whenever you can.

I remember when I first started to do gratitude exercises, I realised that I was repeating the same things I was grateful for every day, and it felt silly. That is normal, even if you repeat the same things every day for the rest of your life, it does not matter, because the journey of gratitude is for you, and you can make it as personal and creative as you like. By focusing on the life's blessings, you can remind yourself when things are not going according to plan.

The last point, *'is it hurting or helping me'*, this really hit home for me. I have been through situations where I have negative thoughts and, in the moment, I ask myself whether the negative thinking is helping or hurting me, it immediately shifts my mindset. If you continuously consider all the negative thoughts that go through your head, it is not a healthy space to be. Being able to remove these thoughts quickly is the easiest way to deal with constant negative thinking. This relates to self-care too.

Being kind to yourself is loving yourself. We need to constantly remind ourselves of self-love and self-care. Putting your needs and wants first. Being mindful of the way you are treated, being mindful of the way you respond to situations. If you start to hurt, you are not helping anyone. In fact, you are making it difficult for yourself. No one else will understand you better than you do.

Resilience transforms, by giving you the confidence to deal with life situations. It helps us redefine our purpose and makes us more conscious of how we manage our life's setbacks.

Self-compassion

Resilience is having self-compassion. To build resilience you must have self-compassion. It is easy to fall and not bounce back, however when you have self-compassion, being resilient gets easy. What you do not want to do is forget the most important person and that is 'you.' Being resilient teaches you this. Without being kind to yourself, you will not be able to do the self-work that you need to do.

Resilience just does not help you deal with low points in your life, it also helps you re-build and transform yourself; have a clear purpose; know your goal in life; and build your confidence, when your self-esteem gets shattered. Rebuilding yourself repeatedly is part of life. How you pursue this is your choice. Only you have the power to decide how you want to deal with life's obstacles. There will be times when staying resilient and keeping faith in yourself, helps you truly aspire for greater heights.

Next time when you have that little negative voice speaking to you, make sure you ask yourself, "is it worth it? is this helping or hurting me." These are exceedingly small exercises that will help you become more resilient. Once you make these minor changes, you will see the differences that will happen in your life. Resilience is the way you make progress in life as it enables you to reflect, and course correct when necessary. It is at our lowest point in life, where you know how strong you truly are, and how strong you potentially can be.

Mastering resilience is not just any skill, but it is a skill for life worth investing your time! Trust me, this is one of the most valuable skills you will cherish forever. No matter what your situation is whether at work or your private life. Resilience will always come into play. It is resilience that will pave the way on how you manage those challenges in life. Resilience is something that should be built from a young age, as it helps build the skills as one gets older, providing us with the confidence needed to deal in life.

If you feel you lack the ability to be resilient, that is okay, that is why you are here to get you started on the journey.

Resilience is all about learning from your experiences, but how can you learn to be more resilient? The more you reflect on yourself and life experiences that is the only way you can grow as a person and build resilience on how you manage those challenging times. You must be flexible and adaptable in your thinking. It is about having a growth mindset. It will give you the confidence and the self-belief to deal with life. People argue resilience is an ability you are born with; be that as it may, whether you are born with it or not, I believe the more you practice resilience the more resilient you become.

You need resilience in your everyday life not just during traumas!

One of the ways you can build resilience is to train your mind to learn how to deal with unique and different situations every day in a systematic and healthy way. This will help you build resilience, so when a situation arises unexpectedly, you will know how to respond.

Psychologists would also suggest 'self-efficacy', which means believing in one's own ability to achieve specific goals. This is an especially important skill to learn when it comes to developing resilience. This involves learning to ignore negative thoughts and self-doubt; learning from your past successes and failures. In this society, too much attention is paid to feel good stuff, rather than serious matters. We do not deal with our failures but hide it away. When it comes to failure, psychologists want you to learn from your failures, it helps your mental growth. Observing failure as a learning curve is an effective way to build resilience.

Like I mentioned earlier on, there is no proven set of steps for learning resilience. However, research has begun to show us that there are links to a set of skills and capacities such as 'self-efficacy' that are resilient responses. It is these sets of skills and capacities that can be developed and improved helping you learn important ways to increase the skill in your life.

MY STORY

Developing resilience is not negotiable. You must persevere to keep moving forward in life. Your mindset is critical to emerging resilient. According to Google, resilience is *'the capacity to recover quickly from difficulties.'* Remember this always. The dark storms will pass, and there will always be a light waiting for you.

I believe what made me resilient in life is my perseverance for not giving up. No matter what life throws at me.

How I build my resilience skills?

I pray, I keep a positive mindset, and I look at the brighter side of things. Bottom line to build your resilience skills, is to maintain consistency in everything that you do.

My advice of steps you can take

1. Speak to someone that you trust; maybe one of your best friends. Someone who will listen, support, and help you in any way they can.
2. Hire a therapist/coach – if you can hire an expert.
3. Begin listening to Podcasts and YouTube videos on personal development, resilience, and other subjects I have mentioned.
4. Read books, lots of them from personal development to spiritual books.
5. Pray and re-connect with God. Re-build your relationship with Him.

6. Start journaling, read your affirmations out loud.

What advice would I give myself when facing calamities?

Now, when I face any calamity, I say to myself, 'You've been through worse weather than this; this is a piece of cake.'

I purposely don't give obstacles and calamities a second thought. I genuinely believe, when I face problems, that if I take a step back, I will see what lessons need to be learnt. What is God trying to show me? What is the purpose of this calamity/trial?

For example, if a loved one has ill health, I ask myself how can I help this person? This person is a blessing in my life, how can I be a blessing in theirs? I try to look for the positives in every situation and I think I do this because of my resilience skills.

Don't get me wrong, I am still human, and get hurt, but I have learnt to look at life's challenges objectively.

A case study

One of my 'clients' got sexually assaulted.

I've seen her go through excruciating pain, the saddest part was she couldn't go to the Police, because she feared the community, and how others will judge her. I did advise her to, but she refused.

However, she picked herself up, and started rebuilding her life again. She was determined not to let the experience ruin her life. She was determined to focus on moving forward with her life and she did exactly that. I am proud of her. Watching her become resilient, inspired, and motivated me to help others who are going through difficult times in their life.

Chapter Six

Repentance

"The world is already filled with so many terrible things, the least you can do is improve yourself, do what it takes and bring joy, peace, and love back into the world."

I tried to find the meaning of repentance; most people have a perception of repentance as being a matter of our feelings, feeling sorry for what you have done, but that is not necessarily what repentance is, it is more than the feeling of 'regret.' You regret some of the decisions you have made in life. Sometimes you may even feel 'remorse', for things that you have done to others - this is not repentance.

Repentance has a unique feature; it is the feeling of what you have done wrong to God. This is quite different from regret. Repentance is overlooked and not necessarily thought through. Repentance has aspects, in Islam it is often described as an action, turning away from self-serving activities, and turning to God. It is about serving and pleasing God. There may be times in your life that you might feel overwhelmed with your past mistakes or the wrong choices you have made in life. This is repentance, practicing repentance gives us **hope**. You spend your life praying and hoping that God forgives you and that all your prayers are accepted. You hope that your prayers are answered and that you live a purposeful and meaningful life.

I really did not understand where to begin with repentance and how it became part of my transformational journey. For me, I felt guilt and shame. I thought God was displeased with me, so, how could I have that conversation with Him? How can I face my mistakes? Until, one day, another light bulb moment when I realised that God loves me no matter what, and He is most merciful and kind. If He does not know my heart than no one can. There was no need for me to feel like I could not be open and honest with God. It might sound silly now, come to think of it, it is. Yet, there were times in my life where I did not feel connected with God... What I eventually learnt is that I must build and invest in my spiritual relationship with God, and it does not happen overnight, it is through the practice of repentance and being consistent in a way the door of repentance opens. The door to your spiritual transformation opens.

True repentance starts from **within**, you must have an open and clear heart before you can start the journey of repentance. In the previous chapters, I spoke about the art of forgiveness and inner healing. If you still have baggage in your life, then practicing repentance is not something you can do straight away. You must remove the toxins and people with toxic energy from your life before you can practise this journey with a clean heart and a clean slate. Re-evaluate your intentions - what is it that you want to achieve; what is your main purpose? It might sound a little selfish, but you are doing this for you so that you become a better version of yourself.

Try not to look at repentance as 'I have nothing to repent of' - let's be honest here, you have something that you should humbly repent of and ask for forgiveness. Sometimes, more than actions, our words hurt people the most. Something you want to 'break' a person, whether that is on a conscious or subconscious level. That is ugly. You must review your actions and your words, it is all about self-reflection, otherwise you will become a passive person, and get away with wrongdoing. That is not fair. When you sin, you put a black spot in your heart, when you do wrong to others, you put a black spot in your heart. By repenting, being remorseful for your wrong doings, is when these black spots are erased from your heart.

Life is a test; you just must try and always look on the bright side. If you are reading this and thinking *"well I am not really the religious type,"* it does not matter because repentance is about reflection and being remorseful of past mistakes, finding a way to put things right, finding a way to not make the same mistakes again.

Practising repentance has helped me to reflect on my inner self. Like everything else, this is a journey that you will have to discover on your own. It is not going to be a perfect journey, but like every journey you must reach that transformation stage if you desire a better life. You must aspire to transform your inner self, and this can only be done through the practice of repentance as one of the spiritual exercises you engage in. This is how you develop your soul, be truly connected with self, truly reflect, and truly embrace the new and transformed version of you.

If you genuinely want to repent, you need to be humble and willing to admit that you do not always do the right thing. Be humble before God and know in your heart that He is right and put your trust in Him. William Osler once said: *"Without faith a man can do nothing, with it all things are possible."* And that is the beauty of repentance; it reinforces our faith in God, humanity, and the universe. If you do not strive to be a better human being, what are the chances of the world becoming a better place? The world is already filled with so many terrible things, the least you can do is improve yourself, do what it takes and bring joy, peace, and love back into the world. As humans you will always make mistakes, say, or do the wrong things but you must come back – return, reflect and stop repeating the same mistakes. It is as simple as that.

There are many benefits repentance can bring you; it opens the door of forgiveness. It enables you to live a life full of purpose and clear objectives. It brings you closer to God, it gives you a chance to be forgiven by God and be in a state of salvation.

So, how do you achieve a high spiritual state? It takes remarkably simple steps and determination. You must be self-disciplined, self-assured and with a little motivation, begin your journey.

How do you start the repentance journey? It is through having the right **mindset**, being able to say to yourself that you are ready to take responsibility for your past and future actions.

- Start with the intention – your intentions speak first before your actions. Having clarity for the reason you want to repent is the start of this process.
- Mindset – you have heard me say this several times, but self-development starts from within, and it starts from how your mind works. Keeping your mindset open, free, and welcoming changes, is a step that will help you get on the journey of repentance.
- Honesty – being honest with yourself is the most important thing you can do. Once you are honest, you will feel a sense of freedom.

- Just repent – pour it all out, let God know that you have reflected and are sincere towards to him. Be honest and speak with him, tell him that you have reflected on all your mistakes, and that you are returning to him. This simple act of repenting means you are turning towards God and asking Him to cover any deficiencies and to help you overcome them.

Repentance equals Transformation

Transformation is about you, not anyone else. Repentance is the chance to change your attitude towards yourself, your outlook on life, past mistakes, and an opportunity to change your relationship towards God. God is a way to keep hope alive. The entire process is a change in your heart and mind, this includes turning away from something that causes you regret towards something that will lift your soul.

If repentance is not something you practise regularly, that is okay! Everything takes time, and repentance is part of your self-healing process. It is an important part of healing, as it is one of the ways you can really reflect and forgive yourself before you can reach the higher transformational stage in your life.

Repentance is an anchor that helps you define what your purpose in life is. I will talk more about this in the next chapter. Coming back to the anchor that shapes you and enables you to reach the highest transformational level that you crave for, many of the things that I spoke about in this book, will help you achieve and 'redefine' your purpose in life. There is not just one element that will help you do this, there are lots of concepts that will help you, some of which I have shared in this book.

We live in a world, where you are constantly pressurised and conditioned into thinking and behaving in a set way. You are designed to think in a certain way, you are conditioned. But if you take the time to analyse, and deeply reflect, you will find deeper meanings and get greater understanding of your purpose for being. I heard about the 'transformational' stage many times but did not really know what it meant until I went through my own personal journey. Until I noticed the change within myself.

My friends and family have noticed the change in me too. That is what makes this journey unique, when you see the transformational work you do and the overwhelming pleasure you get out of it, is truly a proud moment.

Creating vision boards has been a useful tool for me, it gave me a sense of purpose and direction of where I wanted to go in life and how to set the tone for the day. I would make a ritual of doing a little prayer, speak positive affirmations, and look at my vision board first thing in the morning. These were little efforts I consciously made which helped me transform.

You can take small steps by placing reminders around you, for example, you can use sticky notes and write down a few words that inspire you or you can have your vision board saved as your laptop windscreen. The point is, there will be days you might NOT be in the mood to do these activities, but if you keep doing it, eventually it will become part of your life, then it becomes easy. This is where manifestation plays its part. You must believe in the things that you want in your life; it is to visualise your desire and harness the power of your imagination and until it becomes your reality.

Quantum Physics says mind and matter are connected and that it is impossible to separate the two. They are interlinked. When Quantum Physics was first found, the tiny particles the researchers anticipated will separate for example, like electrons and protons, did not. In fact, these particles were expected to behave similar to how planets rotate around the sun. But they did not, instead they responded to the mind. This just goes to show that the mind is interlinked with matter, so also, we know that behaviour is a function of the mind.

Finally, behaviour is how you act and not just with others but with yourself too. Now that I have briefly explained what these three are – repentance, remorse and regret - you can reflect on them to find the present moment.

Ask yourself these:

- What habits do I need to give up? Do I oversleep? Am I often late for meetings? Do I interrupt?
- Do I often think negatively? Do I over think?
- Are there any behaviours I am not proud of? Is my behaviour having an impact on others? If so, how?

The transformational work that you do on yourself is one of the most challenging things you will ever experience, however once you start, you can see the result immediately - in the present and future. Think of it as an investment, you will 'see' the return on investment even though there may be few 'hiccups' here and there. Life will always be that way, but you can only go on to working towards a happy, and peaceful life if you invest in yourself and try now. Nothing good comes without effort. You must give to get.

If you genuinely want the best, then why won't God return the favour? Karma is not just a saying; it is the truth - *whatever goes around comes around.'* You do good, you will see good. That is just the law of the universe. No matter what happens in life, you cannot be bitter towards it as life will show us what you planted. Whether that is something you planted a month ago, or years ago. Our charitable deeds will speak for itself, and our bad deeds will come back to haunt us.

"Always think before you speak" that is what my teacher, Mr Hastings always used to say back in school; those are incredibly wise words. Sometimes you do not know how your words can affect others or hurt others. By taking these initial small steps, you are moving towards transformation. It is the smaller changes that count. If you are thinking of jumping ship to start making big transformational changes, it will not work. Smaller steps help you reflect, making little changes you can manage, a bit at a time.

Always remember one step at a time!

All transformational work is based on what you give back to the universe. Only you can transform yourself, and with your beliefs you will be able to see and experience the richness of the world and see how your actions can make an enormous difference to the world. Jack Canfield[16] talks about imagining a world where you are no longer ruled by your limited mindset and behaviours. A world where you take responsibility for every action and persevere through hardships and challenges making your dreams a reality and refuse to fall victim to the criticisms and abuse of others. Being free from your insecurities and ego; a world where you are kind to others, where you support each other to reach happiness. A world where there is love, joy, and purpose.

---

[16] https://www.jackcanfield.com/blog/powerful-goal-setting-tips/

The kind of reality that you so desperately want, is still within your reach, and it starts with 'you.' If you want to see the world a better place, a world where all of this becomes reality then the biggest contribution, you can make is to change 'you,' live by example, and let your example inspire others to achieve their highest potential.

Some key steps towards transformation I live by:

1. Focus on you first!

To reach maximum greatness, first you must begin to focus on yourself. When it comes down to it, there are three things that a person is in control of and nothing else. These are:

- Your thoughts
- Your visualisation
- Your actions

If you insist on thinking positive things, visualising more successful outcomes, and taking positive steps to achieve those outcomes, you will achieve great results in your personal and professional life. I mentioned this earlier, it is like a domino effect, because others will get inspired and be motivated to get better results in their own lives.

2. Self-improvement commitment

When you make a promise to yourself, you are committing to a life of continuous self-improvement and growth. You develop what is referred to as a growth mindset, where you become curious, innovative, and open to change; it is having a flexible mindset. This makes your life not only meaningful and interesting, but others will be inspired by your dedication towards personal self-improvement and growth.

3. Challenges are opportunities not barriers

We often hear people say they want to transform their lives, but at the first instance of trouble they give up. The road to success will always be paved with obstacles and challenges, it is your approach to these challenges that define you and make you who you are or aspire to be.

When facing a challenge, always see it as an opportunity to grow and gain experience. These moments increase your learning because tough times deliver the most transformative lessons. As a result, people will learn from you, it will motivate them to build the resilience and confidence they need to overcome their challenges.

4. Share your wisdom!

You can share your wisdom and help others learn from your experiences. This can be easily done. By sharing your experiences with others, you help them in profound ways. This is actively facilitating the growth of others. The best gift you can ever give is sharing your success stories which will include your hard times of course; thus helping others achieve more in their own lives.

5. Reach for your dreams!

There are some who simply get stuck and go through life without even trying. You have it in you to succeed, and to create the life that you want. You can do this if you genuinely try to achieve your dreams. Everyone is unique and you can help others by being a notable example. As a great Chinese proverb says: *'helping others is the same as helping the universe.'* Next time, when you go through challenges, learn from them, and help others in the process. You never know what good the universe has got planned for you.

External Transformation

I have talked about internal transformation, now I will talk about external transformation that will also change your life for better. According, to Chinese traditions, feng shui claims that you can use energy forces to harmonise yourself. I am sure you have heard this before: *'you are a product of your own environment.'* If you get the balance and energy right in your environment, you will see how it transforms your life.

The philosophy of feng shui is the practise of arranging furniture in your home and office to create a balance with the natural world to improve your life. Marie Diamond who is a guru in feng shui and recognised name in the field of law of attraction and self-help uses the energy systems of feng shui to help people, teaching hundreds of students worldwide. The core value of feng shui is that it teaches that every object in your surroundings has an influence in your life. By changing your environment, you can promote happiness, good health, wealth, and prosperity.

If you live in an environment full of clutter, all you will promote is chaos and clutter in your life. If you live in an environment where the energy is not flowing, that means there is negative energy that needs to be cleared before you can have all the blessings in your life. Objects in our surroundings bring energy with them that affect you.

This is a 4000-year-old concept that has been proven generation after generation. By altering how energy flows in your home, can transform your life. The easiest way this can be done is by transforming your home and workspace. As you spend most of your time in these two locations, getting the energy flow is essential so you experience external transformation. By implementing few basic feng shui placements you will make your home or office more attractive, and you will earn the benefits of positive and auspicious energy flow.

Now you are learning how to transform yourself externally too. When you start to transform yourself, it starts from within. But you need to look at what transformation you need externally that will help you shape self.

Similarly, in Islam in the month of Ramadan, 'Ashra' which means ten days in Arabic, the first ten days are known as 'days of mercy.' The second ten days are known as 'days of forgiveness' and third ten days are known as 'days of seeking refuge.' Repentance has always played a major role in a person's faith, spirituality, and transformation. It is through repentance you learn from your mistakes and make amends. The more you keep your mind open with a growth mindset, the more you will be able to reach an elevated state of mind. This cannot be achieved with a fixed mindset.

The repentance tool will enable you transform self. You can make this creative and as flexible as possible. It is your journey, and you will need to ensure it meets your needs. Just remember this formula: repentance = transformation

Most of us are in one of these stages and as life goes by, you will gradually move through each stage. Your final stage should be 'enlightenment;' a state of mind surrendered to all mental and emotional judgements and assumptions of life. Nothing is impossible, but the reality is you will have to go through various stages of life to experience every single one of these elements. It is part of your life journey.

This transformation is about 'self-actualisation,' everything you can become. But you can only get there if you repent and take the chance on yourself with making the changes that you need to improve your life. To have a better mindset. To be free from all your fears, worries and limiting self-beliefs. The journey starts within you; no one else has the power to change any of it except you. You have the power to transform your life.

Repentance is not some sort of negative or terrible thing. The word repentance should be seen as a positive connotation. You give meaning to incidents, emotional challenges, and situations in life for which only you are responsible. You see, your life will go in the direction you want it to go. It is through the practice of repentance that you can see the transformational work you do in your life.

My story of repentance

Everyone makes mistakes, big or small. I just needed to repent, and I am so glad I did. It made me humble; it made me focus again on my relationship with God and begin my spiritual journey.

What I did

I was patient with myself, I began learning and growing spiritually. I read, prayed, and surrounded myself with likeminded people. And most importantly, I began being honest with myself, learning about me, understanding me, and tried to be a better human being.

I also started to help others through charity work and the like which gave me a lot of peace and happiness.

What else did I do? Guess what? Did I reach out to people I had offended in the past? Let me tell you more...

OMG, yes! I just remembered and this will sound silly but that is exactly what I did. I started remembering things that I did to others, and I'm talking about things like saying unkind words to school friends. I went onto Facebook, and I apologised to all the people that I thought I had hurt. Even friends that I got into an argument with, I amended these relationships and I sent gifts to people that I thought I'd hurt.

It made me feel so much better, some of my old school friends were surprised to hear from me, but really appreciated it.

I felt good afterwards, and the ones that I couldn't get in touch with, I prayed for, and asked God to forgive me. I did charity donations in their name. so hopefully one day, if I do see them, I can apologise face to face.

Advice to myself if I had to do this over again

Be mindful of your words and actions. Sometimes words hurt us more than actions do.

What would you tell yourself about being Intentional, the Mindset, being Honest, and about Repentance?

They all count, however, it starts with one step at a time.

Always have good **intentions** no matter what, there is always another side to the story.

Positive **mindset** is the ultimate life game changer. What you feed your mind, will happen.

Honest – be honest with yourself, the sooner you are the quicker you can transform yourself.

Repent – it makes you humble, and rebuilds your spirituality.

A case study

Gosh, I can't think of any, but all I will say is that repentance helps you get closer to God. So, if you want your spiritual side uplifted, and want to be closer to God, you know what to do.

CHAPTER SEVEN
FINDING HOPE AGAIN

"Winners are champions and do not go to
battle with the thought that they will lose."

T hroughout this book I have given you the tools and resources
that will help you become a better version of you. Through
forgiving those who offend you, dealing with grievances, and
the benefit of personal development that will make you fulfilled and
your life meaningful, but everything that you have read is related to
having a purpose-driven life. You see, everything makes an impact on
what your perception about your life is, and how you can move on by
not having any grudges with anyone, that is why forgiving others is one
of the ways you can free yourself. You can only do that if you genuinely
want to live a toxic-free life.

Everything in life balances out, and anyone can live life without
meaning, but realise that a life without meaning is a life without hope.
Hope makes you want to get up in the morning. Hope should be your
goal of choice daily. Hope, expectation of a better day, a better life, and
a better tomorrow.

I looked up the meaning of 'hope' from the Cambridge Online Dictionary (COD) and this is what it says:

Hope = 'to want something to happen or to be true, and usually have a good reason to think that it might.'

Why does many refuse or fear to hope? Why have you stayed far from hope?

Could it be because you have hoped in the past and your hope has been dashed? Could it be that you were a few steps from having what you have hoped for, fizzle out right before your eyes? Or maybe you have met a few of your friends who have shared so-called 'hopeless' situations with you; you have believed them and given your traumatic situations and events 'hopeless' as names?

A life without hope is a meaningless life. Just living from day to day as if you are a victim of whatever life throws at you is a dead-end life. I will not encourage you go down that road.

Follow me while I share with you how I built hope back into my life. Let me share with you one of those days when I decided there is better, and I can reach for it. It wasn't easy, but I got through until I found hope. The important thing is, I got there because I knew hope awaited me – and you can get there too.

I gave up on love, I honestly didn't think I would find happiness again. After my experiences, I thought there was no light at the end of the tunnel regarding love. I was scared to step into another relationship, fearful that the turmoil might re-occur, and I just didn't want to find love again. I gave up on men, I honestly didn't believe there were any good men out there for me. I came to a realisation, my father was an amazing man, my uncles, my brothers, they were and are all good men.

So why did I think there weren't any good men out there for me. It is **hope** that made me change my narrative of men. It is my faith and trust in the idea of hope that changed my perception of men. I had to move on, and I moved on with hope and resilience. I didn't want one bad experience take ownership of my happiness. I took ownership of my happiness.

Hope plays a key part when it comes to transformation. You can't change your past, but you can change the now and work towards a better future. It is hope that gives you the control of your transformation journey through acceptance, acknowledgement, and perseverance.

Today I am grateful to be in a place of contentment, peace, and happiness.

Throughout my personal transformation journey, I have read many books, articles, and research papers that have helped me tremendously. I have learnt how to believe in myself, I have learnt how to **transform**. I did it all on my own, well, not really, I had God helping me and without Him I wouldn't be here.

There will be times in life where you might feel stuck in a dark place. I want to assure you that you can find hope again, you can find happiness again. The doors of opportunity and abundance are always open to you, and you should learn how to get to and through that door. It is possible.

Losing my father at such a young age, and going through a horrendous marriage, I found life does not stop. You make it what you want it to be. You have the power to change and make things happen. You can transform.

Next, I want to tell you a little bit about mental health and how it relates to hope and resilience. After that, I shall share a few other significant lessons I learnt.

Mental Health

Allow me to add one more very important aspect of personal development – mental health, NOT mental ill-health.

According to usatoday.com,

"… decades of research show hope is a robust predictor of mental health. Not only does it make life more enjoyable, experts say, but hope also provides resilience against things like post-traumatic stress disorder, anxiety, depression, and suicidal ideation."

Hope is non-negotiable. In terms of developing resilience, you will find that hope is a component of resilience. Resilience is not found in one who has no hope. However, mental health is vital because both require that one thinks right. If you want to be great, remember this, greatness does not bow to hopelessness.

You see, no matter what happens in your life, no matter the chaos and pain you experience, if you still have life (and you do because you are reading this), you still have access to hope and resilience if you are willing to develop both. But to do this, your mindset needs to be intact and strong.

Your mental health is your responsibility and I wonder if you have ever thought about the beauty of that. You probably have never thought that it is a beautiful thing to be in control of your own thoughts. Let me explain. When you are not in control, that means someone else is in control. The beauty is in being able to choose what you think and control what you think in order to flourish.

Therefore, to maintain a strong mental health so that you develop hope and resilience, you must, and I say, must take control of what you think, your mindsets. I have said this in many ways throughout the book. And yes, I know, it is the hardest thing to do but it must be done if you are to live the life of a winner. Winners are champions and <u>do not go to battle with the thought that they will lose.</u> They have won before they don the armoury for war, before they leave home; before they get to the camp and arraign for battle; before they ever wield the sword. The battle is already won in their thoughts so that their minds are win-ready.

James Allen puts it this way in his book, 'As a man thinketh:' "in all human affairs there are efforts, and there are results, and the strength of the effort is the measure of the result."

I could not have said that better.

How about you? How do you begin anything? With the thought to win, lose or just do it? Choose to win; this is a decision only you can make.

I know you have been taught that you cannot control the outcome, but I tell you, you are in control of you. And that is all you need to control - **you**. Because frankly, you cannot control anyone or anything else. Just as no one can control what you choose to think.

Think **hope**.

Think **resilience**.

See what happens.

Snyder, (2000) in Yıldırım and Arslan,(2020) defines "hope as one's perceived ability and capacity to achieve a goal with positive motivational state." While Fredrickson et al., (2003) in Yildirim and Arslan (2020)[17]

---

[17] Yıldırım, M. and Arslan, G., 2020. Exploring the associations between resilience, dispositional hope, preventive behaviours, subjective well-being, and psychological health among adults during early stage of COVID-19. *Current psychology*, pp.1-11.[17]

define hope as "an emotional process of psychological force or buffer that strengthens individuals to be resilient and help them to cope with disturbances."

One refers to hope as an 'ability' while the other as a 'force.' Both are correct. You have the ability and once developed, it is a force in you.

Go on, take control of what you **think**, quit allowing any and every thought pervade your mind. Take control because you can. Your mental health is a critical element of transformation from within.

6 Significant lessons

Some important lessons that I have learnt so far in my life, and I say 'so far' because there is still so much to learn, are:

Lesson 1: Humans evolve

Humans are always evolving; you just need to take a moment to reflect and realise that this life is all about transformation. While you are transforming so are others around you. Allow them to. You are your own business so focus on you and evolve, transform into the best you possible. You are your own business.

Lesson 2: Control your thoughts, your mindset

This is the most important lesson in all of life. You should always have control over your mind by deliberately deciding on the thoughts you allow to take a space in your heart because they (thoughts) set your mind. Regardless of what may be going on around you, regardless of the challenges you may be facing right now, you choose what to tell yourself, you choose what you think about what's happening, and this determines how you feel. Happiness doesn't depend on any external event or force, rather it depends on what you're thinking and how you are controlling your mindsets.

Lesson 3: Everything has a purpose

Finding your purpose is finding what God created you here for. You matter. There is a timetable and limit for eating and drinking, finding your purpose is limitless and you must ask yourself what your priorities in life are and once you know what these are, keep them as priority. Your purpose determines the kind of life you live.

Lesson 4: Focus on the now

Ekhhart Tolle, the author of '*The Power of Now*: *A guide to spiritual enlightenment*[18]' – was inspired by Stoicism and Marcus Aurelius. They both state the importance of focusing on the present, on now. Focusing on the present and giving it your all is done by taking each action as if it were your last, you will notice the difference in your performance because you will always be doing your best. If you want to see it from a spiritual standpoint, you can view this as there is no guarantee of a tomorrow so you might as well give it your best shot. It is this best shot, it is this 'now' that will give you the significant booster you need in life.

Lesson 5: Constantly dig deep

If there is nowhere you can go, you know there is always yourself that you can count on. Find space to think, have 'me time,' everyone

---

[18] Tolle. E, (2001), *The power of now*, Yellow Kite

knows, should know or can find out where they can go and have that time for deep inner thinking.

Lesson 6: Dealing with obstacles

Your mind knows how to adapt and convert obstacles to steppingstones. So, all you must do is turn the obstacle around. Take a deep breath. Take the time to understand the obstacle. There will be tribulation if you are on earth, but you must remember, there is a message in every obstacle. Find what that message is, find what it is that you need to learn from the experience.

So, where does one begin finding hope again? I wish I could give you a black or white answer. That won't be right. The truth is, there isn't a straightforward answer. But what I do know is, no matter what happened in my life, I never gave up. This is what has kept me going, that is what gave me **hope – that there is a better life ahead somewhere and I will find it, I will get there.**

If you are in a dark place in your life right now, finding hope may seem impossible. But let me assure you once you go through this book, chapter after chapter, page after page, all the topics I spoke about are related to finding 'hope' and you will. Just do the work, the rest will follow.

What is hope, everyone will have a different definition of hope. My definition of hope is – *trusting the process.* You see, without trust, there is no hope. Once you give something 100%, giving it your all, you will begin to have hope again.

There were times in my life where I didn't have anything to look forward to, but I was hope-full and I knew if I gave my personal development 100%, I knew the sky would be the limit. There is no one in my way.

I know, trust me, I know the feeling of knocked down, hitting rock bottom and not able to see the light. But strive, you must and fight you shall. It's been almost ten years now since I started this transformational personal development journey, and this isn't my first book. There are many more that I have written but never managed to finish, why? Procrastination. It's easy to fall into the procrastination trap, the little evil twin voices telling you, "You can't do it; you are not good enough!" The one that eats you up slowly. Fight it! You are better than that.

Nothing and no one can define you. Only YOU can make decisions for your life. It is in your hands. So is finding hope. There will be people telling you all sorts of things like: "you can't do this because you are a woman, you can't do that." Let people talk, you just do **you**, and do what makes **you** happy.

As you have gone through this book, I hope you have gleaned some knowledge you can use to help you along with your transformational journey, while realising the number of things you can do to help yourself. Some of the points that I touched upon for example, dodging the bullet, dealing with inner blips are all things I wish I knew earlier on in life. This is my journey. Having gone on this journey, I know better, and I am, perhaps, a little wiser.

You are responsible for your own happiness. I am here to show you a few paths you can take to get there. I hope that I have done it justice. When I was going through my struggles, I wished someone just gave me a book to read.

I hope after you read this book, you can help someone else by giving them this book to help them deal with their struggles.

Thank you for being part of my transformational journey.

Cheers to yours.

Finally, in this part of the last chapter, I want to give you a bit more insight into my marriage now.

I have got some questions I think you, my reader, might want to ask me and I have answered in as much detail as I can. I hope these bless you.

1. What happened to cause you to hope again regarding men?

My father was an amazing role model, recalling how he conducted himself and lived; he was a man of great stature, dignity, and honour. I knew my dad would never let me put up with a man like my ex. To be honest, he never would have arranged a marriage to him. My father would never have wanted me to be miserable, he had been through a lot in life. But he made sure he filled his daughters' lives with love and happiness. He would have wanted me to be happy and to re-marry and start my life again.

All the men in my family i.e. uncles, brothers etc are all good men. So, I knew there was hope out there for me. I just needed to stay positive and believe that I was going to find a good person.

2. How did you meet him?

We met online, that's another book altogether.

Straight after I got divorced, my family did try to arrange another marriage. Although I appreciated their gesture, I knew that I couldn't go through an arranged marriage a second time. I knew that I wanted to marry for love, I wanted to get to know the person rather than marry a stranger. I wanted to marry someone that I knew!!

Meeting men became tedious. Where do Muslim divorced women go to meet Muslim men? It's not like you can attend social gatherings, even if you do, there's religious and social segregation between men and women. So, it was very difficult meeting someone. It's not like Bollywood movies where you just bump into your dream guy. It wasn't like that at all.

3. Did you hesitate or brush him off?

It was different. When I first met him, it was comfortable like we had known each other for a while. It was easy. Our conversation flowed. He was serious and wanted to get married and so did I.

4. Did any family or friend react to your new relationship - good or bad? If so, who and how?

I think my family were over the moon. Like I said, they wanted me to re-marry. So, when I found someone else, they were happy. They made sure that we were both ready for marriage and in a way, they probably felt guilty for getting me married to my ex. Although, I never ever blamed them, it wasn't a forced marriage I still had a say whether I wanted to marry my ex or not. I think they understood that I didn't want to go through another "arranged marriage". I was done with that.

Few family members, elderly aunties and uncles, were a bit disappointed with me because I think they thought I would change and marry someone of their choice rather than a man of my choice.

But they got over it once they realised, I would not change my mind.

5. How did you respond to them?

I stood my ground. I made it clear that no one was going to arrange my marriage. I was adamant that I didn't want to go through that experience again.

6. What is different about you now in this marriage compared to the first? What did you change, or have you changed about yourself?

I feel like I'm wiser in this relationship. I feel like I have a better understanding of what a relationship is all about and what it entails. Marriage is hard work and needs a lot of work. I'm a totally different person to whom I used to be. Learning about mental health and studying psychology really helped me better understand relationships, and most importantly, myself. I dealt with all my baggage, my inner grief, insecurities and trauma. I feel fresh and revitalised now.

7. How many years after your divorce did you meet him? Were those years difficult for you?

I think I met him about two years later. I would avoid going to family functions - weddings etc. I avoided people as much as possible. I just didn't like the constant questioning and pitiful comments. It was exhausting. I just concentrated on my personal development. Go to work, gym, study - I concentrated on ME.

8. Is he of the same culture and background as you?

No, he is of a different culture. He is from Turkey, but we are both Muslims. I knew I could compromise on culture but not on religion. I wanted to marry someone from the same faith as me.

9. Have you had to deal with any similar issues as in your first marriage? If so, what and how did you handle it differently?

I am not going to lie; we do have our moments like most couples. I suppose I've learnt how to handle disagreements better now. Whereas before, I would just "freeze;" now, I take a step away, breathe and talk about it when we've both calmed down.

Finally, I would like to say this about my husband:

My husband is my best friend and a good man. Through these past years, there have been many compromises and things that we needed to work on as a couple. We did it, we both worked on it, and still work on it. There's always something that I'm either learning about him or from him.

When I go on about my "psychology" jargon, he may not necessarily agree with everything, but he listens and tries to see my point of view.

We are always doing our best to encourage and support one another, making each other feel loved. We are both growing individually and together. That's important - being on the same page.

Most importantly we have fun together. It doesn't feel like hard work. It feels natural, being able to be myself. I can't imagine my life without him.

And I'm grateful to God that He has made this possible.

MY STORY

I think being a divorcee in my close knit South Asian community was hard, really, really tough. There is always stigma, and many women just like me who have been through the same ordeal know what I am talking about. It's not easy, there's a lot of cultural pressure, added to the marriage break up. It's easier for men, they seem to get away with everything but not women.

What I did

I decided to rise! I was on a mission to personal success. I knew that I was responsible for my own happiness and no one else, if the community doesn't accept me so be it.

I began to focus on my life making real changes. Thus began my journey of hope. I launched my coaching business - **@respirecoaching (Instagram)** - and began to help women from my community, through non-judgmental support as they developed hope, resilience, and most important, strong mental health. I gave them a 'safe space,' something that I didn't have when I was going through my struggles.

What I would do differently

I would grow 'thick skin' as the phrase goes. Let people talk, Subhana, you focus on your life and happiness. Start dreaming, why not? I am entitled to everything I desire; I deserve happiness and so does everyone else. I would change my mindset from the onset.

A case study

https://www.bbc.co.uk/news/world-us-canada-62427084

This article really hit home! Unfortunately, this is common within southeast Asian Muslim communities and it's happening in the West too, right outside our doorsteps.

Women are often stigmatised, blamed, shamed, and victimised. This is unfair. Sania Khan was another woman like me, who wanted out of her marriage. But society didn't let her, they tarnished her. It makes you wonder how many other vulnerable women are out there.

Well, there you have it. I have shared with you as candidly as I can my journey of resilience and hope, my journey of transformation from within.

Start YOUR'transformation from within' journey. You will be a better person not just for you but for family, friends, and society at large.

Stay blessed!

Printed in Great Britain
by Amazon

86412987R00071